AFFILIATE

MARKETING

JONATHAN BECKER

Table of Contents

INTRODUCTION TO AFFILIATE MARKETING

What is Affiliate marketing?

Affiliate marketing is the process of earning a commission by promoting other people's (or company's) products. You find a product you like, promote it to others and earn a piece of the profit for each sale that you make.

Affiliate marketers sell other peoples products on the web and they get paid a commission for every sale they make. No contract, no requirements or budget is needed to start. All you need is a computer with an internet connection.

Let's say you have some experience in affiliate marketing and you want to speed things up: Do not invest your money in software of any kind, but in knowledge. Don't buy fish, learn how to fish!

Affiliate marketing is a successful business tactic that many companies use to boost their sales and to acquire more revenue. Business takes advantage of affiliate marketing to increase advertising as well. If you want to use affiliate marketing, then pay close attention to the helpful tips that you will find in this book.

Pre-sell the offers that you want your readers to buy. Just

adding a link to a product is not going to make you much money. Explain why you love the product and why you are someone they should listen to. Include the benefits that you have received from the products.

Be a seller, not a salesman. There is nothing that turns a customer off more than being thrown gimmicks and sales pitches continuously. Have respect for your consumer and recognize that if you subtly discuss the product well enough, you will have people interested in buying it. Don't force it on them.

If you do not have your own website to promote affiliate products on, then create one. A website is a great place to communicate with potential buyers and market affiliate products. On the website include relevant articles, useful product reviews and your contact information so that customers can get in touch.

Nothing destroys a visitor's opinion of a website owner faster than a concealed advertisement. This does not mean that it is impossible to satisfy visitors and engage in affiliate marketing; the honest webmaster is simply honest and transparent about it. Visitors should always be made aware when a website gets money for endorsing a particular product. They rarely resent a straightforward advertisement as they do a duplicitous one.

A great affiliate marketing tip is to reduce the amount of clutter on your site. You want visitors to notice the content and the ads. Having a lot of extra stuff such as calendars and clocks can distract visitors and can prevent them from clicking on what you want them to click on.

A great affiliate marketing tip is to take time to understand your market. Try to see where others have failed and then create a solution to those problems. If you can come up with a solution to a problem, you'll have an opportunity to promote an affiliate product.

Beginning Affiliate Marketing

Getting started with affiliate marketing might not be a bed of roses initially.

Even if visitors don't make a purchase immediately, almost all programs offer cookie duration, normally consisting of 30 - 90 days. What this means is that as long as the visitors have the cookie in their cache, you'll still receive a profit from the sale.

You still need to create some kind of traffic using your affiliate links to make the sales. The good part is that there are ways to generate traffic without the need for your own website or domain.

One time thief is searching for and investigating possible affiliate programs. Online companies like ClickBank and Commission Junction make your work much easier as they have compiled large amounts of publishers that would like people like you to help sell their products and services.

The most commonly used source for affiliate marketing is probably ClickBank. They offer a special interface for locating good affiliate programs, the marketplace. But it is a bit too rigid in what it offers to really allow for the powerful searches and number crunching needed to pick the top affiliate programs you should promote.

A product like CB Affiliate Revenue makes your life as an affiliate marketer working with ClickBank much easier, and it will save you a lot of time that would be better spent on other money making tasks.

Affiliate tracking can also be a problem. Once you have applied to become an affiliate for a company, they'll usually supply you with a personalized link or code. It's very important that you implement this code into your page correctly, or you may be sending visitors to the company without receiving any profit. CB Affiliate Revenue will help you do this when working with ClickBank.

Majority of snippets in the code will contain a unique user ID, which the company uses to distinguish which site sent traffic.

Make sure you take notes when you find a good affiliate program. Write down where you found it, when you started to use it, any login information you may need to get back to your affiliate information, your affiliate ID (and/or urls) and where you use the link to send prospects to the publisher.

You will need all this information further on in your affiliate marketing career; and as the number of affiliate programs you join increases, so does the risk of forgetting where it came from.

Key to an Online Income Booster

There are numerous ways to make quick money online. One can earn from a few hundreds of dollars to a few thousands per month, in fact some smart individuals are making thousands of dollars in one day. For those who look at this virtual world of internet as a money making platform, it becomes a virtual play ground for them. It's really easy to make some great money online provided you have some knowledge of internet and some basic understanding of SEO which is more specifically termed as Search Engine Optimization, keyword research etc. Out of hundreds of ways to make a quick buck online Affiliate Marketing Program is one of them.

Now it's very important to understand what exactly this Affiliate Marketing Program is? It's a program that helps in growing market share along with a boost in virtual recognition on the internet resulting in elevated bottom line profits. In simple language an affiliate marketing system is a way to promote a product or service over the internet that results in generating good traffic to a website which would finally help in increasing a sale of a product or service offered on that particular website which would generate online income in form of commissions on the final sale for an Affiliate. The means to promote products and services can be a normal website, a blog, an online store which is live on internet.

9

Basic Understanding of affiliate marketing

The idea of Affiliate Marketing Program has been lingering around for a long time over the internet since it's an excellent way of making quick money online. Affiliate marketing system has great potentials to make quick riches if incorporated in a right way, however many people now a days are involved in this virtual money making activity making just a few hundred dollars a month which is very low and the reason behind this is that they somehow do not pay attention to small details that would help drive traffic to a website and result in making more and more sales every month.

When someone decides to get involved in affiliate marketing program by promoting different products and services online, there are two different options available. One is to promote without having own website, by simply finding the products and services that are to be promoted, and driving traffic to the landing page of a website where these products and services are being sold and this can be done through social networking, articles, blogs etc. Another best way to do this is having one's own website, making it search engine optimized by finding and incorporating right keywords in the website content making it more search engine friendly and having ads of those products and services appear on your website.

In either ways, affiliate marketing program can work and make some good money by generating commissions on final sales. But it is always advisable to follow the second option since it will result.

In generating lot of income online and that too on a complete autopilot whereas the first option is a temporary way that can be adopted for a short period of time.

Here are some steps that can be followed to establish a great affiliate marketing network program.

First of all, it is very important to identify where on internet can these products and services that offer commissions on sale be found? The answer is simple, there are hundreds of websites that allow merchants to post ads that would attract affiliates to promote their products or services and earn good commissions.

A domain name for a website needs to be purchased and hosting needs to be arranged for the same. Again, there are several websites on the internet that offer domain names and hosting services at reasonable prices.

An attractive webpage needs to be created or this can also be done by someone who knows how to do this. Being attractive does not mean having more graphics or glittering fonts, rather a webpage with very simple design but with lot of meaningful content enriched with right keywords looks more attractive to search engines.

After a webpage is setup, ads for promoting products and services as an affiliate can be incorporated in it so that it clearly becomes visible on your webpage and gives an option to visitors to go ahead and click on them.

Now at this step, it is really important to realize that just having a webpage setup with interesting content in it does not automatically drive traffic. To obtain precious time and email addresses of visitors to come and see your webpage, it has to offer something of value that is factual and would make a visitor feel that it worth visiting your web page. It can be a mini course, a free guide, an eBook, discount coupons, etc. and you can trade all this stuff on your webpage by just asking for a visitor's name and email address to subscribe for newsletters through an opt-in form which would help you in list building.

After following all the steps mentioned above correctly, making money online with very little efforts is guaranteed.

Affiliate program businesses are still on a roll as the boom in the affiliate industry continues. Many are part of this industry, and many more want to enter it, either as merchants or as affiliates. The world of affiliate business continues to change and everyone needs to adapt to these changes to be able to stay in the business. The best way to have the ability to go with the radical flow of affiliating is to have firm grasp of the fundamentals. The basics of putting up and operating an affiliate program business are vital to success.

Affiliate Program Business Introduction

A website is the flag that signifies the company it belongs to. In the past, only the well established and highly profitable companies have their own websites. But nowadays, thanks to the continuous evolution of the Internet, setting up a website has become so easy anyone can do actually do it. The fastest and easiest way of building a website is by using an online website builder that has ready-made templates and other webpage elements you can choose from to construct your very own unique website design. These sites will also be the ones to provide your sites URL for you. The downside to using these site builders is that most of them attach advertisements on webpages that are made with them, and their greatest advantage is the ability to design a website and get it online in less than an hour.

Design only grabs the attention of human readers, but before people can marvel at the beauty and greatness of your sites appearance, they must first be able to find it. And for people to find your site, the best and fastest way is that they find it in the results page of the major search engines. And one of the best ways you can get good rankings on the trusted search engines is through search engine optimization or SEO. SEO however can prove to be complex and hard to do especially to those who have never even heard of it before. A good alternative to SEO in getting your website seen is engaging in an affiliate program. Such action allows you to profit from your content-driven website's traffic as well as make sales with the same website.

An affiliate program sometimes also called associate program in layman's terms is a system of arrangements in which an online website known as a merchant website pays affiliate websites commissions to send traffic to it. The affiliate websites post links to divert the traffic they receive to the merchant site. They are then paid depending on the affiliate agreement. The commissions may be based on the number of visitors the affiliate site sends to the merchant site, the number of people the affiliate site sends to the merchant site and clicks at least one of the product advertisements, or the number of visitors directed to the merchant site by the affiliate site and actually makes a purchase. The framework of the agreement is that the merchant pays according to the agreement the associate whenever his affiliate site brings site traffic or money to the merchant website. The recruitment of affiliates is not only a great way to sell products over the internet but it is also a great marketing strategy as it provides the merchant website a unique competitive advantage. Networking can be said to be one of the best and most effective ways to get your site famous online.

There are at least three parties in an affiliate program transaction:

1. The Customer

2. The Affiliate Site

3. The Merchant Site

The concept of having an affiliate program business which utilizes the World Wide Web as a marketing strategy was first announced to the public in 1996 by Amazon.com CEO and Founder Jeff Bezos. Amazon.com encourages affiliates to post links to the Amazon website in general or to specific books. Whenever someone clicks on the link and makes a purchase the affiliate who owns the link will receive a certain pre-agreed percentage of the earnings. All the affiliate need to do is to send traffic, and the rest is done by Amazon.com like order taking, money collection and product shipment. Amazon.com is not only the first affiliate program business; it is also on of the most successful with more than half a million affiliate websites.

Over the years affiliate programs have grown to epic proportions and have taken many different forms. Affiliate program businesses are now everywhere and they are found in almost every niche of the business world. Many companies specializing in e-commerce now function as merchants while those who do little or totally no e-commerce work as affiliates.

Affiliate Program Business Basic Payment Methods

There are three basic types of affiliate program payment arrangements:

1. Pay-Per-Sale (Cost-Per-Sale)

The pay-per-sale agreement has been popularized by the mother of affiliate program businesses Amazon.com. Under cost-per-sale the affiliate is earns commissions from the merchant each time he sends a customer to the merchant website and that customer makes an actual purchase. Amazon and many others pay a specific percentage of the sale as commission while others pay a fixed rate for every sale.

2. Pay-Per-Click (Cost-Per-Click)

Pay-Per-Click is considered by many as the most popular and common affiliate agreement. Under such agreement affiliates are paid fixed rates based on the number of visitors who click on the links placed on the affiliate website that lead to the merchant website. A purchase is not required to earn commissions, all that has to be done is that the visitor clicks the link and stays for a certain time usually at least 30 seconds on the merchant website. Whatever the visitor does once he gets to the merchant site does not affect the commission.

3. Pay-Per-Lead (Cost-Per-Lead)

Under the pay-per-lead arrangement affiliates are paid based of how many visitors they send to the merchant website and subsequently sign up as leads. Signing up as leads means that the visitors fill out the information request form at the merchant site. Leads are used as targets for conversion into customers or are simply sold to other companies which are in search of leads.

Affiliate Program Business Other Payment Methods

A company sets up an affiliate program based on its needs. Therefore, it is very usual for a company to have an affiliate agreement having some variations with the basic payment methods. There are also three common variations of affiliate program payment methods.

1. Two - tier programs

Affiliate program businesses that offer two-tier agreements profit through sales recruitment and commission sales hence thy have a structure similar to network marketing business or multilevel marketing organizations. In addition to the traditional commissions based on sales, clicks or leads facilitated by the affiliate's site, commissions based on the activity or productivity of referred affiliate sites are also received.

2. Residual Programs

Affiliates under this arrangement are continuously paid commissions if the visitors they get to go to the merchant website also continue to make purchases of products and services from the merchant. This kind of arrangement is usually utilized by online merchants who require regular payments usually on a monthly basis from their customers.

3. Pay-Per-Impression (Cost-Per-Impression)

Online merchants who make use of this arrangement which is also sometimes referred to as pay-per-view pays commissions according to the number of visitors affiliates can cause to see the merchant's banner ad. Such arrangement has been developed as an advertising strategy but has now been adopted as an affiliate strategy.

The reduced risk is the biggest advantage of the payment methods utilized by affiliate program businesses because a merchant pays out commissions only when its desired results are met. Traditional advertising like television and radio ads as well as online banner ads are relatively risky on the part of the advertiser because they are like placing their money on a bet that the advertisements will be effective and achieve whatever they are suppose to achieve. The ad is considered as a success when it brings to the merchant more money than what was spent, but this is unfortunately not always the case. With affiliate programs on the other hand, the online merchant only pays out commissions when things are going the way he wants them. It is far easier for websites to join affiliate programs than it is for them to attract advertisers but much less risky for merchants.

Affiliate Program Business Administration

Affiliate programs are relatively simple and easy to manage, all they need is some dedication and patience because there should always be someone tracking the actual activity of all affiliate's links to be able to provide them proper commissions.

Advantages of Affiliate Marketing

Affiliate marketing, when done correctly, can be extremely beneficial for both the affiliate and the publisher. Here are six advantages of affiliate marketing from both sides.

1. Don't need to have your own product

A lot of people don't have the time, money or expertise to create their own product, so affiliate marketing is a great way to make money off other people's hard work. This also means an affiliate doesn't have to worry about researching the market to find what people want. Instead they only have to find which products are selling well.

2. No customer support required

Anyone who has ever had their own product will tell you that customer support is one of the worst parts of running a business. Affiliates get to keep their share of the profits without ever having to worry about being in contact with the customers. All the problems are dealt with by the publishers customer support department.

3. Only a small investment required

There aren't many business models which allow you to start up with virtually no investment, but affiliate marketing can be one of them. When using free traffic the only investment is time. Of course, there are paid methods of traffic generation also, but in general becoming an affiliate marketer is a low cost business with the potential of being very profitable.

4. Working from home

It's many people's dream to work from home and only when they feel like it. Affiliate marketing isn't paid on an hourly rate so you can choose the hours you want to work. Some people do affiliate marketing as a hobby, others as a full time job. The beauty is it's completely up to the individual. It is important to remember though that the more effort you put into affiliate marketing the greater the rewards in most cases.

5. A much greater audience will be exposed to the product

One of the main advantages for a publisher who has an affiliate program is that the affiliates have the potential to reach a much wider audience then he or she ever could on their own. This means there can be many more sales than there would have been if the publisher was the only person promoting the product, for a relatively small amount of extra effort.

6. Less effort needed to drive traffic

Getting traffic to a website can be a time consuming process, so to have a large amount of affiliates doing this for you is a huge advantage for any publisher. By using affiliates the publisher has to spend less time worrying about getting people to the sales page leaving more time for other areas of the business. Leveraging other people's effort for your own business is a great way to make a lot of money.

There are many advantages of internet marketing for both the affiliate and the publisher which is why it has proven to be such a successful business model. Affiliate marketing has generated many people a healthy income.

Common data an affiliate program business should always be aware of are as follows.

1. The number of people who click on the merchant site's link on an affiliate site.

2. The number of people who end up buying something or performing some other predetermined action once the affiliate sends them to the merchant site.

3. The number of people who see the merchant site's banner link on an affiliate site.

4. The original arrangement between the merchant and each affiliate as well as changes if any.

Both merchant and affiliates need a lot of effort to enter the affiliate industry. Merchants need to actively seek and recruit affiliates while affiliates need to actively search for affiliate programs they might be interested in. Many huge and successful affiliate programs like Amazon.com even deal with their affiliates directly because the benefits they reap from their associates are more than worth direct administration. Such companies are in complete control of the payout process and the merchant is the sole entity that determines the amount of commission each affiliate will receive. In spite of this fact, these companies still attract a lot of associates due to the fact that there is no real risk or cost in their program. Affiliates simply put links up and wait for commissions.

Affiliate Program Business Networks

Affiliate networks composed of affiliate brokers serve as mediators between merchants and affiliate program websites and affiliates. They assist the associates put up the links in their websites and also track all the activity of these links as well as arrange all payments. Affiliate networks are also beneficial to merchants in the sense that they help recruit affiliates by including the merchant's website in their online affiliate program directory. Help centers and report centrals are the common features of affiliate networks though additional features may vary.

Affiliate networks are most beneficial to aspiring affiliates because through them a wide variety of affiliate programs become available in one central location making finding a good and suitable program that fits your site much easier. Affiliate networks of course, as payment for the convenience they serve take a certain cut on each transaction they facilitate which is usually around 20% of the affiliate commission.

Any type of website can involve itself into an affiliate program though most affiliate network service agreements forbid offensive and pornographic content. Successful affiliate program businesses though referred to as merchants do not even need to make sales to gain profits. Content based affiliate businesses in fact get most of their earnings from advertisers which where attracted into advertising on the merchant website because of the high volume of traffic its affiliates are sending to it; hence there is direct conversion of traffic into profit. Pay-per-click affiliate programs are one of the most efficient means of increasing traffic.

It can be said that there are as many kinds of affiliates as there are types of businesses. Generally, any website from top sites to personal pages can take part in an affiliate program, and with the correct choices can earn themselves some money. There also exist affiliate businesses which are just actually huge collections of many affiliate programs. These sites operate by joining a lot of pay-per-click or pay-per-lead advertisement programs and then offer their visitors a portion of the commission they receive on each click or offer them a chance to win big rewards.

Becoming an Affiliate Program Businessman

The first choice for anyone wanting to involve himself in affiliate programs is whether to be a merchant or an affiliate or both. Setting up an affiliate program and becoming an affiliate merchant is the best choice for those who operate an e-commerce site and desire to imprcve their sales. Becoming an affiliate of several merchants is the best choice on the other hand for people who own small content sites and run them only as a hobby. The choice is likely to be influenced by the budget and the element of affiliate programs what suites your website the most.

Entering an affiliate program as an associate is quite easy. Just go to the merchant website and fill out the online affiliate application form. The form is likely to ask of your name, address, desired payment method and other personal information as well as information on your website like URL, name, and content description and then of course have you agree to the merchant's service agreement. Affiliate networks are generally free.

Once you receive the approval of the affiliate network you are then ready to start selecting the affiliate programs that interest you. Since most affiliate programs accept affiliates at no cost al all, it is best to immediately discard all programs than charge membership fees. Once selection is complete, the merchants you have selected will then review our site and once they accept your site they will guide you step by step on the process of appropriately posting links. Payment arrangements will also be finalized during this guide. Most affiliate programs require associates to reach a minimum earning threshold before they release commissions because of the fact that the amount an affiliate earns per transaction is relatively small. This means that no payment will be received by the affiliate until he reaches the particular minimum amount. After everything is set up and all has been explained to you, you can then start working on your website to help you earn more money.

Real Results from Affiliate Marketing - What You Should Know

Often the newbie to marketing on line gets involved with affiliate marketing. The reason for this is that it is fairly easy to do and can be done with a minimum amount of tools and relatively little effort. While affiliate marketing can generate substantial income, the way to achieve real results is by using it to springboard your own product creation efforts.

Basically affiliate marketing is the process where you generate visitors to a merchant's site and get paid when the visitor makes a purchase from the merchant. That purchase results in a commission to you. In essence, an affiliate marketer is a salesperson that receives a commission when a sale takes place.

In my experience, the new affiliate marketer should focus on selling info-based products. The reason for this is that typically the purchaser of the product is looking for a solution to a problem. Usually an instant solution. And usually that instant solution can be provided by the information contained in the product being sold.

The added reason for focusing on info based products is that the affiliate marketer can then create their own competing product if they discover that the product being promoted generates profits. This is not possible if, say, you are selling a physical product like a camera.

One of the biggest mistakes the new affiliate marketer makes his not having a mechanism for capturing leads (sometimes referred to as prospects). The way to capture lead is typically through a vehicle called a squeeze page. The reason the vehicle is called a squeeze page is because you are "squeezing" the visitor for his or her e-mail address in exchange for promised information.

If the affiliate marketer is building a list of leads, it then becomes easy to recommend products to those leads. Eventually those products will be the products created by the affiliate marketer. This is when the affiliate marketer turns into a product developer and product creator and starts selling his/her own information products.

Therefore, the true way to achieve real results from

affiliate marketing is to use affiliate marketing to test the profitability of products, generate leads, and then sell those leads your own products. This will produce real results from your affiliate marketing efforts.

Simple Strategies for Affiliate Marketing Success

It always surprises me how much money you can make by selling other people's stuff on the Internet.

The real numbers never truly hit you until you fill out your taxes.

You can be your own boss, work your own hours, carry out your business from anywhere in the world you want to live. You can create automatic marketing systems that work 24/7/365 days of the year.

Earn money even when you're sleeping, vacationing or out enjoying a gourmet meal at your favorite restaurant. Total freedom. So is it any wonder then why I am constantly analyzing my whole marketing structure to figure out what is working and what is not working? Finding out just what strategies are giving me the best returns on my efforts and time. And I am constantly trying to discover just what I can do to increase my affiliate sales and online traffic.

It basically means breaking down your online marketing into its core elements and examining each one with close scrutiny. What can be improved? What can be eliminated? What needs to be redesigned?

Any serious online marketer must be actively working on these core elements to stay competitive in the Affiliate game.

With these thoughts in mind, here are some simple marketing strategies that can affect and contribute to your success for selling affiliate products on the web. Marketing factors that should always be at the back of your mind, influencing your every move.

Quality Content

People use the web to find quality content or information. Always remember this fact and apply it to each step of your marketing plan - give your visitors quality content and you will succeed online.

There are no ironclad guarantees, but get this one step right and you will probably make money online.

Design your website and your web pages around quality content. Useful, relevant content will give people a reason to come to your site and also give them a reason to return. Provide good information first and let the sale or selling be secondary. People do not like a pushy salesperson, not in real life and not on the web. Develop a friendly, helpful relationship with your potential customer and you will succeed.

Keyword Driven

The Internet is keyword driven. These are words or phrases people type into search engines to find what they're looking for on the web. They are also your keys to online success if you're going the SEO route, picking the right keywords will be your main starting point.

Professional marketers use keyword software like Brad Callen's Keyword Elite to research and find their profitable keywords, but there are many free tools/sites which you can find online to help you do your keyword research -- Seobook.com is a good one.

Daily monitoring of your major keywords is also important to keeping them in the top positions. Any movement downwards should spark more link and/or content building immediately.

Keep in mind, Google, which controls 60 percent of the web's search traffic, is also a great source of information on your keywords. Use Google to search the sites in the top 10 spots for your keywords; also check Google for the Paid Ads related to your keywords and monitor these ads over a period of time to see which ones are profitable. Do your keyword homework and your affiliate marketing will be a lot easier.

Niche Focused

If you're into affiliate marketing, you must concentrate your efforts on small niche markets where the competition is not too stiff. Choosing the right niche markets is vital to your affiliate success. Demand should be high and/or you're selling a high-ticket custom item.

Once you have chosen your particular niches, concentrate on dominating these in all the search engines. But don't forget that the fastest and sometimes the most profitable way to tackle a niche is through PPC (Pay Per Click) advertising, especially if there is little or low bidding on your keywords. Google AdWords, Yahoo Marketing, MicroSoftAdCenter... should be explored and tried.

List Building

The power is always in the list. Make sure you collect the contact information of your site's visitors. Offer freeebooks, guides, special deals or bonuses... to get your prospects to opt-in to your AR follow-up systems.

Studies have shown that people usually don't buy until the six or seventh follow-up. I like building hundreds of micro-lists for all my major promoted affiliate products. These follow-ups with specialized information and special deals, coupons and bonuses will increase your sales.

Have Multiple Income Streams

Don't be dependent on just one product at one price to generate all your income. If you just sell just one product with no add-ons or up-sells your prospects will not have enough choices to pick from. Conversely, if you try and sell too many products you may confuse your customers and they'll buy nothing. A successful affiliate marketer will have a good mix of related products that provide different income streams.

Build Relationships With your Prospects

An affiliate marketer expert will 'tell rather than sell'. The main value of an affiliate marketer to any prospect is somebody who provides information. It's how a prospect will come to trust your opinion. It's what will make then open and read your emails. It will bring them back to your website and it's what will motivate them to click on your affiliate links to make a purchase.

Traffic

Obviously, traffic is one of the key elements to earning money online mainly because without traffic you're dead in the water. You must explore all avenues to generate targeted traffic to your affiliate links.

These sources are always changing; blogging and social bookmark sites are very important now. So too are video and audio formats so make sure you use them in your marketing.

Article marketing has worked extremely well for me and it is, along with search traffic, the main reason I can earn income online. A simple marketing technique that still works because articles will bring targeted traffic to your site or sites.

33

One of the Best Ways to Generate Leads for Affiliate Marketing Is Solo Ads

Many of you might know about solo ads and for some it might be a new term. Many affiliate marketers use this source of traffic and lead generation activity. It is a well rewarding business model.

What is Solo Ad and how it works?

Solo ads, work best with Email Advertisement, in which you need to prepare an email template or campaign and send it across to the list owner and the list owner than send that email to subscribers and you pay some amount for that service. You can add your product, service or affiliate link in your email and list owner, send traffic to that email and you get very high targeted traffic on that email and Link.

Let's say you have a product or you are promoting someone else product as an affiliate and your targeted niche is health & fitness then you contact the person who have a massive email subscriber list of health & fitness niche. You discuss with him/her and come with a fixed rate per click or visitor then he/she will send your email to all the subscribers from that specific niche who is actually interested in your product. This is how it works. It's very much in demand and very profitable. Let's see more in detailed.

1. Find the Affiliate Product and Niche.

If you are interested in affiliate marketing and do not want to create your own product then promote someone else product in the beginning. You need to find the best product which is high in demand and also make sure it is competitive. What you need to do initially is to go for low cost product so that you get more idea and you might get the first sale quick to build-up your confidence. High end product might take long time and as a beginner it will not be easy to get the first sale that quick.

2. Look for Seller

Once you choose the product then you need to choose the Solo ads Seller. You need to be careful here. It is a very tricky part, but you will learn step by step. There are many ways to find the good sellers in the market just go to Google and search for best ad sellers for affiliate marketing promotion and you will have lists of many reputed ones. What you need to do is use your product nature + Solo ad seller in Google.

Here are some examples;

Fitness Program Solo Ads Sellers

Fat Lose Solo Ads Sellers

Email Marketing Solo Ads Sellers

Make money online Solo Ads Sellers

This way you can have many good numbers of seller list and then you contact them and ask for numbers of Subscriber, Reviews, testimonials, Price etc. There is one more way to find them is Advertising agencies. There are many good ones out there.

3. How to target the affiliate link?

Once you choose the best seller of your interest now it's time to prepare the campaign to share with the seller. The main question here is should we target direct link to affiliate product or not?

If you send the traffic directly to affiliate link, then you cannot make your own subscriber list. You can do this, but you will not have your own list ever.

You can create your own landing page with email subscribing so that the visitor comes to your landing page and fill in the email and then you can send your affiliate link directly to them. This way you can build your own list.

Finally once you decided how to target your affiliate link, then send an Email campaign to Solo Ads seller and he/she will email that to all the subscribers and you can relax and track & Monitor the clicks & Sales.

Conversion Rates Are Crucial

In affiliate marketing or in any kind of marketing, your conversion rates are crucial to your success. You can get all the targeted traffic you want but if you can't turn those visitors into a sale, it's game over.

Your sales pages or content must convert into a sale in order for you to succeed. With affiliate marketing it is a little trickier because not only do your pages have to "pre-sell" the affiliate product but the landing page/site where you send that traffic must also convert into a sale.

However, I have discovered one of the keys to high conversion rates has nothing to do with landing pages, sales pitches, etc., but has to do mainly with which products that you decide to promote. You must thoroughlyresearch your affiliate products and ONLY promote the top quality brands in your niche and you will have much better success. Also choosing products that are only available online will increase your conversion numbers; so too will promoting products that offer special discount coupons and deals.

Multiple Streams & Residual Income

Any serious online marketer will leverage their traffic and marketing by promoting many different products and services. They will develop different sources of income from their sites with affiliate links, Google AdSense, paid advertising, partnerships... are all used to develop multiple streams of income. If one should dry up, there are countless others still producing income.

I have found the major third-party affiliate networks like Commission Junction, LinkShare, Shareasale, Affiliate Window, Amazon are really good for finding and promoting products online. These sites will handle all the record keeping and sales stats for you. Plus, they send your monthly checks to you like clockwork. All you have to worry about is providing quality traffic to your affiliate links.

However, like any professional marketer, I save my special promotions and efforts to affiliate products or services that will give me a high return on my marketing efforts. Mainly, I only promote high-ticket items or products that will give me residual income. Make one sale; get paid time and time again. I also like forming partnerships with companies so that I get a percentage of the sales for the life of any client I refer. Those arrangements have special priority for the obvious reason they give me long-term residual income.

You Must Test Everything.

You must constantly test and track what is working and what is not. Which traffic is converting? Which keywords are converting? Which products are converting? Which niches are profitable?... you simply must TEST and KNOW which factors are working in your online marketing structure. Unless you test and track everything you will be marketing blind, and that's no way to run an online business.

I have found Google Analytics to be extremely helpful for testing and improving your conversion rates. I am also a firm believer in the daily reading of your traffic logs and stats... these places will show you where the real money is hiding. Use this information to improve your traffic and sales.

Like any endeavor, the more knowledge you have, the more successful you will be in reaching your goals. This is especially true for affiliate marketing on the web. And always remember, affiliate marketing does take some work and time to set-up, but the rewards are extremely rewarding.

Best Popular and Famous Highly Paying Affiliate Programs

Affiliation is an automated and robotized marketing program where an online website advertiser, merchant or entrepreneur engage webmasters (the person who keeps a specific website) to place their banners ads or buttons on their blog or websites. Webmasters will receive a referral fee or commission from sales when the customer has clicked the affiliate link to get to the merchant's website to perform the desired action.

Generally, make a purchase or fill out a contact form, desired action varies from merchant to merchant and according to their offers or promotions. In other words, we can say that, it's an online business center for thousands of affiliate programs on the web. Now a days, affiliate marketing has become a multi-billion dollar industry and it's the best way to monetize your blog or website. All the affiliate network systems have their own tracking, reporting, and payment system.

Affiliate programs or associate programs is an agreement between an advertiser and a webmasters, if a company or organization has generated, produced or designed a product and they are promoting and trading it via your website then you can also generate extra income by inviting your website visitors to promote it in exchange for a commission.

Moreover, if you are monetizing your website or blog with the absolute affiliate program then it can make a lot of money with a slight effort. For this, you need a healthy, bountiful and rich content website with a handsome amount of targeted traffic.Advertisers finance in affiliate programs for initiation of consumer interest or inquiry into their products or services of a business, it is also called lead generation. Different advertisers provide different kinds of affiliate programs. All affiliate plans do not work in the same way or pay the same rates. If you join a search engine affiliate program you most likely w ll be placing text links or banners to their advertisers and you'll work on a pay-per-click fee. Similarly, some of others allow you to set up a shopping or store page that offers products related to the content of your website.

Basically, in association of any affiliate merchant means you are paid a commission per sale on the advertiser's website and pay-per-click affiliate programs reward the minimum amount, as affiliates are usually paid per thousand clicks (CPC).

There are lots of other affiliate marketing programs than the ones that have been mentioned below, but these are the ones that are extremely successful.

1. CJ Affiliate by Conversant (Commission Junction) - Since 1998

Minimum Payment Amount: $50, $100 (Direct Deposit, Check)

Payment Method: Check, Direct Deposit

Programs Offered: CPA, CPL, CPS, CPC

Referral Program: No

CJ Affiliate by Conversant is an extensive, largest and highly paying affiliate marketing network in North America, it operates globally. CJ Affiliate is one of the oldest advertising company that is why it is preferred affiliate network of more than 500 companies and major online stores on the internet. I will recommend it personally because it has unmatched hub of advertisers, beautiful and easy to understand user interface, unworried payment system and the customer support that we cannot find anywhere.

CJ Affiliate has a very large variety of products to promote and merchants (advertisers) frequently pay high amount of commission rates for CJ publishers when we compare to other marketing affiliate companies or even their personal in-house affiliate program.

CJ Affiliate Network is free to join and you can simply sign in to CJ Account Manager once your application is approved and apply to different affiliate programs. Some of the advertisers approve publishers immediately while others approve manually after reviewing your account/website. But you need to link a quality website with healthy and rich content to get approval for individual affiliate programs.

2. ShareASale - Since 2000

Minimum Payment Amount: $50

Payment Method: Check, Direct Deposit

Programs Offered: CPA, CPL, CPS, CPC

Referral Program: Yes

ShareASale is another popular and most accepted affiliate network with a large amount of product choices. It has collected an excellent ratings, with the company's outstanding persona, safety, morality, customer service, and ease of commission payment receiving glowing reviews. In fact, it is the well-known affiliate marketing company with over 3,900 merchant programs and more than 40 different categories. There are lots of other affiliate programs on the internet that are very distinctive to ShareASale.

ShareASale also provides you an extra feature that you can add products to your "basket". It means, you can keep all information about specific merchants or products that you'd like to apply for, review, or export later on.

If someone is unfitted or failed to find an appropriate advertiser on CJ then most apparently it will be here at ShareASale. Moreover, to get start joint affiliate program with ShareASale is not complicated. There are couple of important and easy steps to get started. Essentially, you have to verify that you own your website before you can join any of them, which involves placing a key code in your website's header tag.

3. Rakuten Affiliate Network - Since 1996

Minimum Payment Amount: $50

Payment Method: Check, Direct Deposit, PayPal

Programs Offered: CPA, CPL, CPS, CPC

Referral Program: No

According to writers and online surveys, Rakuten Affiliate Network Company has been declared and listed in one of the largest affiliate network, with over 10 million affiliate partnerships. Rakuten Affiliate took the number one spot in the 2012 Affiliate Networks because of platform stability, support quality and ability to spread all around the world with more than 4,000 affiliate programs which allows you to manage your own program using the company's various service and support options.

Rakuten is not the quickest to sign-up or the simplest to navigate, but there's a lot of helpful guidance as you go. You have to sign-up with each separate advertiser before you can boost their products. This reveals that quality is important here.

Rakuten Affiliate has a lot of physical products to promote, including some big-brands. They provide access to thousands of publishers recruited daily worldwide. Search by product category, traffic, consumer geograohy and other criteria significant and relevant to your online affiliate campaign. They provide patented tracking technology, easy tools to upload ad links, coupon links or product feeds and reliable online payment options.

4. AWIN.com (Affiliate Window) - Since 2000

Minimum Payment Amount: $20/£20

Payment Method: Check, Direct Deposit, Wire Transfer

Programs Offered: CPA, CPL, CPS, CPC

Referral Program: Yes

AWIN.com, Affiliate Window is one of the best affiliate network in Europe and prominently increasing around the globe with over 2,100 advertiser and 75,000 publisher respectively. It provides instance access to nearly 77 sectors in 11 territories. This affiliate program is at the top because of its unique traffic light system which is providing visibility on payments, low threshold payments available in multiple currencies twice a month, simple user-friendly platform, interface with real-time reporting.

In 2013, UK buyers made 150M purchases via affiliate websites. Monetize your website and join the thousands of bloggers by adopting affiliate marketing as a way of monetizing your website in an intelligent and excellent way.

Affiliate Window is incredible to work with because this affiliate program understand that independent publishers have different demands and will work with the advertiser and publisher to ensure the program works for both. It has dedicated publisher services team with sector specialists, access to more than half of the UK's biggest brands* (as listed by IMRG 2013 survey), live chat support and multiple range of tools to create links.

5. Click Bank - Since 1998

Minimum Payment Amount: $10

Payment Method: Check, Direct Deposit, Wire Transfer

Sell Products: Globally

Referral Program: Yes

Click bank a well-known affiliate network and has a huge statistics with 200 million customers, it features over 6 million digital products, such as e-books, software and membership sites. With their network of 500,000 digital marketing experts in over 190 countries, digital product will reach customers around the world. They help you to set commissions that maximize the network of digital marketers promoting your offers and together watch your sales grow. Click Bank has delivered lifestyle products to customers around the globe.

After joining Click Bank affiliate program, you can get up to 75% commission on all sales. Find particular informational lifestyle products with just one click, obtain advice on any topic, immediately access products and there is no need to wait.

ClickBank sells lifestyle products that are produced by fervent entrepreneurs. Their products give innovation and instruction on topics ranging from training the family dog and Paleo cooking recipes to workouts to become a better surfer. With each click and every sale their products improve the lives of customers around the world. They stand behind the products and strive to deliver unparalleled customer satisfaction.

6. Zanox - Since 2000

Minimum Payment Amount: €25

Payment Method: Check, Direct Deposit, Wire Transfer

Programs Offered: CPA, CPL, CPS, CPC

Referral Program: No

Perhaps the largest European network and a partner of Affiliate Window and eprofessional, zanox supports more than 4,300 international advertisers in the successful marketing of products and services on the internet. However, it is not very much familiar with USA but has a growing terrific reputation gradually. Globally, more than 700 people work for zanox and its partner companies. Moreover, zanox champions the establishment of international quality standards with its own Code of Conduct for all participants in the network.

Affiliate networks becomes important when they have an exclusive relationship with a brand. The most famous handmade marketplace Etsy.com's affiliate program is powered by Zanox. So you will need a Zanox publisher account to become an affiliate of Etsy.

Simply, display ads on your website and earn money for generating sales and leads. You gain maximum reach via Zanox global publisher network with a wide variety of publisher models. You will be given maximum benefit from their global network of high-quality brands and attractive promotions and their statistics enable you to track and improve your performance. They also provide great importance to trust, network quality and transparency.

7.Affiliate.com - Since 2008

Minimum Payment Amount: $100

Payment Method: Check, Wire, ACH, PayPal

Programs Offered: CPA, CPL, CPS

Referral Program: Yes

Affiliate.com only works with top and high quality affiliates and provide some of the most sought after campaigns across various verticals, including campaigns for more than 100 different countries. They provide world class affiliate support, whether you are looking for a particular offer or are in need of a fresh new creative, their affiliate managers are your number one resource for helping you to generate the highest level of revenue. Lots of other affiliate networks suffer from disconnection, not so from this network.

Affiliate.com oblige anyone from beginner level to advanced affiliates. They have a very helpful staff that take each case on an individual basis. So, if you do not have much experience yet you should probably be best to try one of the other networks first.

Affiliate.com network declares more than 2,000 live campaigns in different categories, so there is definitely a large selection to choose from. To become a part of Affiliate.com you have to fill out an affiliate application form, your application will be reviewed within 2 business days. You'll get a call to confirm all of your information and be assigned to an affiliate manager. They also offer domain parking and redirect monetization services.

8. VigLink - Since 2009

Minimum Payment Amount: $10

Payment Method: PayPal

Programs Offered: CPA, CPL, CPS, CPC

Referral Program: Yes

It is very much similar to Skimlinks, complete the sign up process and then simply add one line of code to your website or blog and VigLink will automatically turns existing links on your pages into revenue generating links. VigLink can also insert new links on relevant terms and phrases to capture purchase purpose. You can also earn from purchase intent created in your app, the content created and shared over mobile apps drives purchase. VigLink's Rest API opens up a new revenue stream for publishers by allowing them to earn from this created purchase intent.

VigLink manages a publisher network of over 2 million sites and apps, as well as an advertiser network of over 50,000 brands and merchants. It is also backed by top investors including Google Ventures, Emergence Capital, and RRE.

VigLink believes that it links out every feasibility so what seems to be a simple and normal link to you can be turned into a monetizing affiliated link with them. It takes a 25% cut of the affiliate commissions generated from your website or blog. You get 35% of what they earn for a year from your referral. Moreover, VigLink identifies commercial products mentioned within content and links them to destinations determined in real-time, advertiser-bid auctions.

9. Valuleads - Since 2009

Minimum Payment Amount: $50

Payment Method: PayPal, Pay Check, ACH (Direct)

Programs Offered: CPA, CPL, CPS

Referral Program: Yes

ValuLeads is an energetic and widely growing, achievement based advertising agency founded in 2009. Their basic goal as a team is to provide the best value possible to every organization they work with. ValuLeads understand that each client, whether advertiser or publisher, has different needs and wishes. Therefore, they work with their customers on a one-on-one basis to create a completely customized system or campaign designed to maximize value and results. ValuLeads is committed to getting the top payout for each and every campaign.

At ValuLeads, every publisher in the network is distributes as though it were their most important customer. No matter, what the size of your campaign, they will always provide you the best possible support and guide you through all the ups and downs.

They also offer on-time payments, as well as flexible payment options and provide weekly payments (for qualified publishers). At ValuLeads dedicated experts and quality service continues from 8 A.M until 12 A.M, seven days a week. Fill out an application to set up a free consultation an affiliate manager will call you to discuss what offers to run, and how to work together to make you some money. They also offer referral program.

10. JV Zoo - Since 2009

Minimum Payment Amount: $50

Payment Method: PayPal, Stripe or Authorize.net

Programs Offered: CPA, CPL, CPS

Referral Program: Yes

It is free to become an affiliate at JVZoo. It provides one affiliate link and instant access for all products in a sales funnel. JVZoo having little resemblance to ClickBank.

Because, it's a network for affiliates and sellers based around digital products. It's easy to manage, just like with ClickBank, you can check out the marketplace to get an idea of the products you could promote before you have even signed up. After joining, you can have access to the JVZoo Affiliate Product Library, which contains products from a wide variety of categories.

Their affiliate product library gives you up to the minute conversion and EPC details for all products. Know what you can expect from a promotion by seeing network wide performance data. When you promote a vendor's product, you are automatically cookied for all of that vendor's products.

As an affiliate, see exactly how your campaigns are accomplish in real time. You can even generate multiple trackers for the matching product, using our Tracking ID System. You can keep an eye on your campaigns with an instant sales notifications. Notices are sent to your email's inbox each time an affiliate sale is made. Vendors deal directly with buyers, so there is no need to provide customer support for people that purchase from your affiliate link.

How to Choose the Right Affiliate Marketing Program?

Robert Kiyosaki's Rich Dad Poor Dad has made being your boss a very popular concept. Everybody wants to be their own boss. You make money for yourself, you do not have to report to anyone and you can choose when not to work. What's there not to like? However, most of us are stuck in our jobs as we have to pay the bills.

Affiliate Marketing is a great way to start being your own boss, while you still keep your day job. The risk is low. You only require a few hundred dollars to get started. It does not require much time. You can start by committing only one to two hours a day to your Affiliate Marketing business.

As a beginner, it is important to choose the right Affiliate Marketing program. A good program can save you lots of time, and make you more money. Here is the top tip, when choosing an Affiliate Marketing program:

Pay for a comprehensive step by step program

Most marketers will tell you affiliate products are free. You should not be paying for them.

Yes, it is true that affiliate products are free. Any affiliate program that asks you to pay for the products you are selling is a scam. So why am I asking you to pay for a program?

When you first get started, you might get lucky and stumble upon good affiliate products. The best places to look for them are merchant sites like ClickBank. Now that you have gotten your top-selling affiliate product to promote, what do you do next?

Most new Affiliate Marketers have NO CLUE where to start. How to set up your own websites, squeeze page, autoresponders and other technical requirements? How to drive traffic to your website? These are things that you can learn eventually if you spend hours and hours scouring the Internet. That is assuming you know what to look for of course.

But why waste your time and effort? Invest a few hundred dollars on a step by step system, and save some time and effort. Use the time you have saved, to apply what you have learnt and recoup your investment.

The key is to ensure that the system you choose is comprehensive. It has to cover two basic aspects. Firstly, it has to teach you how to set up the technical aspects of your Affiliate Marketing business. You need to know how to set up your website. You need to know how to change your website. You need to know how to set up your Autoresponder. These are 3 basic technical requirements that the program should teach.

Secondly, the program should teach you how to do marketing and drive traffic to your website. Look for gurus who have proven results. Don't just take their word for it. Look for signs of their success. How do they dress? What car(s) do they drive? Speak to their past students and hear what they have to say. If everything points to real success, you've got a winner!

Once you have signed up for a good program, follow it strictly. Most Affiliate Marketers fail not because they don't know what to do, but because they don't work hard enough and give up to quickly. Stick to your program and work at it religiously.

How Do You Choose an Affiliate Program

So you are one of those millions of people who want to work at home, you have done some research and like the idea of the support and benefits affiliate marketing offers. You like the fact that the products are provided, together with training and other perks to start you earning commissions quickly; even without a website. You have been searching Google for programs but there are so many to choose from, you are in a quandary already!

Here are some guidelines to help you:

If you choose a topic you are really interested in, passionate even, you will be keen to work with your business and each day will be exciting watching it grow. You will want to recommend your products to like-minded people to help them learn more, meanwhile you will be learning too.

Here are some profitable niches you may be interested in:

- Making or saving money
- Personal development
- Weight loss
- Health and fitness
- Golf or some other sport

Work in an area you would really like to learn more about and you will have a dream job, it won't seem like work. You will be one of the few lucky people who have achieved their dream.

Do some homework by searching for the best programs in your chosen field. Look at the individual programs and see what is offered to new affiliates. All programs have different incentives.

What is the commission structure like? Are there some high-end products available in the range and some entry-level products. With high price, high value items you don't have to sell so many to make a good income. They are not necessarily harder to sell, if they are good value and what people are looking for.

What training is on offer? Is it produced in an easy to understand format, is it up to date? What other support is available?

How well-known is the company, is it a household name? Do they already have a big following?

Is there a forum, Facebook page or community group, you can join for support if you wish to? What support mechanism do they offer newbies?

Find out as much as you can before you join, read reviews etc.

Find a good coach or coaching system that suits your style of learning, this will make learning the new techniques easier than trying to work alone. Information over oad is a situation that hits new affiliates, plus the frustration of not knowing who to turn to, or what to do next. This can create thoughts of giving up and could make you abandon your new venture; resist negative thoughts and gain encouragement from your group.

With a good coach you will work a tried and tested formula that is proven to work. You will be learning tasks in the best order. Your product, sales pages and training are provided. Everything will be professionally prepared and the products will be a range of best sellers.

With the help and support of your coach you will soon start to earn commissions, whilst you are learning the techniques. Begin in your spare-time as it will be a while before your income matches your day-job, but you are on your way to an exciting future with time and location freedom and the satisfaction of developing your own business.

Affiliate Marketing Mistakes To Avoid

We all make mistakes. It's part of the process of learning. But some mistakes are greater than others. Take affiliate marketing as an example.

It's considered to be the easiest and quickest way to make money online. Yet for some people it just doesn't work. The concept is pretty straight forward. As an affiliate marketer you earn commissions by promoting other people's products or services on the internet. You find a product you like, promote it to a target audience, and earn a piece of the profit for each sale that you make.

So where do people go wrong. Here are 5 common affiliate marketing mistakes to avoid.

1. Don't Expect Instant Success

Affiliate marketing online can generate revenue fairly quickly. Having said that, a life-changing income won't happen overnight. It takes time to build an audience and a customer base. If you accept that making money with affiliate marketing is a legitimate business model you'll realize that you have to put appropriate business strategies in place to succeed and these take time to implement.

2. Don't Target A Large Generic Audience

You'll have more success if you target a smaller niche market rather than a massive market. For example, 'weight loss' is a massive market. But 'weight loss for women over 40' is much more niche and targeted. The most successful affiliates directly target a specific niche market which a product or service that is designed for people in that market.

3. Don't Give Up Too Quickly

Affiliate marketing is a competitive business. And many people give up right when they are on the brink of developing of success. You can make a profit from affiliate marketing but you need to take a long-term view and commit to a least 1 or 2 years to build up your business.

4. Don't Promote Anything and Everything

Restrict yourself to a handful of high-value products that have good reviews by customers. Don't just promote all and every affiliate program that pays out high commissions. Promoting anything and everything, with a new offer going out to your email list or website visitors every day, is a quick way to get dismissed by your audience.

5. Don't Be Like Every Other Affiliate

Don't forget that there are many other affiliates promoting the same products and services you are.To encourage people to buy from you, rather than another affiliate, create a bonus, such as an eBook, report or video that someone would be happy to pay for. By doing this you add value to the purchase, something that the majority of other affiliate marketers never do.

Your job as an affiliate is to help consumers find the products they need. You're the liaison between searching and solutions. But the online business world is a vast marketplace and it's easy to drown in, try to play your role in a strategic way.

How to Create a Successful Affiliate Marketing Campaign: Advice From Experts

Affiliate marketing has emerged to be one of the most effective ways of monetizing online content. Although there are many true stories of individuals who have made small fortunes through affiliate marketing, this straightforward concept isn't as easy as it seems.

Here are tips on how to create a successful affiliate marketing campaign:

Select Your Niche

One of the most common mistakes made by people who are new to affiliate marketing is targeting a broad swath of the most lucrative and popular services and products. This makes it almost impossible to generate enough sustainable and relevant traffic to compete consistently. You can start off on a good note by choosing a type of content that you are interested in and capable of producing. You will then come up with a comprehensive plan for promoting relevant, in-demand products in your niche.

Search engines have been making changes on how they rank content, giving priority to high-quality content. This means that the best way to achieve lasting success is to become a reliable source of insight and information on topics that are natural to refer.

Create Valuable Content

A good program shifts away from pay-per-click marketing strategies and focuses on a specific target audience. The best way to establish productive relationships online is by delivering high-quality content. In short, this is what attracts the audience to your specific channel, makes them come back again and establishes a level of trust that helps your consumers feel comfortable to play a role in your campaign.

By providing your consumers with information that compels them to take action and make an informed purchasing decision, you become a valuable resource. They will return more often and share your content with their network.

Cross-Channel Promotion

While an important element of an effective content strategy for an affiliate marketing program is to make use of SEO best practices and copywriting to get search engine traffic, only a few can be successful without cross-channel marketing. A constant flow of traffic is what powers and affiliate marketing campaign and the best way to increase exposure, expand your reach and establish deeper connections is through cross-channel marketing.

Use Software Tools to Enhance Efficiency

It goes without saying that it is small details that make it difficult to run an affiliate marketing campaign. Online publishers and entrepreneurs who are getting started take their time to understand how certain software tools work to reduce the workload of running the campaigns and providing accuracy and insight in monetizing your content.

By using a solution that helps you link the right products to your blog, website or social media pages and provides all the tools you need to optimize, track and analyze your affiliate relations, you can be confident that you will get a stream of income from the campaigns.

Know Your Legal Obligations

Today, marketers are required to follow certain legal guidelines that govern how businesses are conducted online. The same way, affiliate marketing has areas of compliance that must be adhered to and understood.

While anyone involved in this marketing program is required to familiarize himself with current FTC regulations, it is important that you understand that any party that is involved in an affiliate relationship is required to make full disclosure. A good affiliate market works to win the support and trust of his audience. Let your audience know that you make money when they click on your affiliate link, and also that you give a good review for brands and products you endorse for free.

Guide to Make Money through affiliate marketing

Affiliate marketing today as a strong internet marketing tool is one easy and lucrative way to make money online. But the major reason why most newbies affiliate marketers fail to benefit from the program is because they do not know where to start and most of the product out there that they have bought assume they already know everything about internet marketing.

The trick to succeeding online with affiliate programs is more than finding a profitable product to promote but rather it require your "mental toughness". Most internet marketing guru which you have bought there product will never tell you this, but will rather set you up for failure by the claims of instant income that will pours into your bank account the minute you buy their product.

QUI

Here is what I mean.

The moment you start to implement what is inside their product and you are not rich overnight, you start to feel that you have failed. But don't quit yet; succeeding online require your mental toughness. If you want to make endless cash flow of income with affiliate marketing you should be mentally tough and focus minded. You should be able to put in extra hours and fight through the days of no sales.

Affiliate marketing is not a get rich quick scheme or a push button system to solve all of your financial problem. But if however, you are willing to put the work in and follows a system that has proven to be successful, then you are not far from your first affiliate sales.

The formula to succeeding online with affiliate marketing is having the right knowledge together with focus which will hasten your plan of action.

Here is the break down:

Knowledge + Focus = Actions and Actions = Lots of sales.

Making money with affiliate marketing is super easy if you are better equipped with life changing powerful money making blueprint that has proven to work.

Affiliate marketing simple tricks

Securing reciprocal links is a modest but important step in any profitable affiliate marketing program. Website owners should always do what they can to get a link from their affiliates back to their own website. Such links are doubly desirable because they not only increase the utility of the affiliate program, they also improve the website's standing in search engine results rankings.

Look for companies that are willing to pay extra for your time spent. Some affiliate businesses expect you to design the marketing tools you will be using to get them buyers. Finding a business that is willing to pay you for the extra efforts is quite a bonus. If you are spending your time for their sales you should be paid for it!

Take your time and try different approaches to figure out the best way to promote your affiliate links. Don't just take the first option you see. Study the different choices carefully and test out different ads to see which ones get the best results. Rotating your ads frequently can help draw more attention.

When promoting a product as part of an affiliate marketing program, you will see the most benefit out of showing your readers how the product specifically benefits them. Just because something is a good product doesn't mean your readers care about it. You need to give specific examples as to why this particular product is something they need in order to get them to buy.

Affiliate marketing is a niche market that allows you to make money using the Internet. If you have access to a computer regularly, have online capabilities, can follow simple directions, and want to make money in your spare time, affiliate marketing is for you. Companies are more than happy for the advertisement.

A great affiliate marketing tip is to provide your real name and a working email address to your visitors and customers. Providing your name and email address will make you look credible, and you want to look as credible as possible in order to gain the trust of your visitors.

Check the company's affiliate program to make sure they use tracking cookies. You want to make sure that if a customer visits their website the first time through you but doesn't make a purchase until later, you receive credit for the purchase they make. You want to make sure you get all the credit you are entitled to receive.

JONATHAN BECKER

Advanced Affiliate Marketing Techniques

When choosing affiliate products to promote with your Internet marketing business, you want to pick products that cost more so that you make a higher commission per sale.

But you also want to have a whole range of products at different price points so you can keep people buying no matter how much or how little money they have.

For example, let's say you pick self-help as your niche. You should have a bunch of products that cost less than $10 - such as eBooks or video courses - because a lot of people seeking to improve themselves don't have a lot of money but still want to buy something that will make them better people.

The 'Profit Ladder'

Then you should have more expensive products in the $10 to $100 range so that you can offer them to people with more money to spend and also push your customers up the profit ladder. That means getting people to buy increasingly expensive products.

Then you should have some products that are really

expensive, such as those that cost $1,000 or more. This is to appeal to people who have a lot of money to spend but also to have a big money offer that people can aspire to. A lot of times these types of products are things like personal coaching, or seminars people can attend to become masters at whatever it is they want.

Big money products not only satisfy people's desire to get the best there is, but also provide you with the biggest commissions so you can make the most money even if you only make a few sales.

Niche Statistics

Popularity of Niches

Before you start promoting affiliate products, you want to make sure the products or the niches you choose to work in are popular. You don't want to waste your time working in niches that there aren't a lot of customers. Instead, maximize your potential revenues by only working in the best niches that have scads of customers.

So how do you find out what niches are popular? Like anything else these days, you simply use the internet. There are plenty of places you can go to measure the popularity of a particular niche. The first place I always recommend is Google Hot Trends which lists the top 100 searches on Google during the previous 25 minutes.

Researching Niche Statistics Online

Google is the largest search engine and is used by more people than any other, so it is a reliable source to tell you what is hot at the present moment. Another site is Yahoo Buzz, which also shows the top searches but on Yahoo, which uses the Bing search engine. Yahoo Buzz also gives a little more information than Google.

Two other similar sites are Trend Hunter and Trend Watching. These are more geared toward consumer goods, such as electronics, appliances and other hard goods rather than digital products, which are what you probably will be promoting.

Sources for Niche Data

ClickBank has a lot of information about the products it offers. A similar site that also has lot of data you can use to measure popularity is Commission Junction.

With the affiliate products you promote on ClickBank and Commission Junction, you make a commission every time somebody clicks through and buys that product.

The Importance of Social Media In Affiliate Marketing

Unless you're made of money there's only so much you can do with PPC advertising alone. Eventually then affiliate marketing comes down to being able to promote your website and your brand and to reach a wider audience. This means leveraging the mailing list, blog and social media accounts that you have set up and using them to attract more new visitors and to build trust and authority. What you need to recognize here is that you are the 'middle man' in any business the 'middle man' is effectively unnecessary. The buyer doesn't really need you and the seller doesn't really need you, so you need to make yourself indispensable to each. In this case, that means helping the product creator to sell a far greater number of products than they otherwise could. And for the buyer, it means providing great quality content and information and helping to find the best deals and products out there. Every business is ultimately predicated around providing value of one kind or another. This is how the internet marketer provides their value. At the same time, it's also how you succeed as an internet marketer and how you build momentum and a following.

In this chapter, we will see this link very clearly while looking at the three main types of marketing available to you to promote your brand.

Things You Didn't Know About Affiliate Marketing

Affiliate marketing is basically referring people to various products and services around the internet. For each sale you generate through your affiliate link, you earn a commission. The size of the commission depends on the products themselves, who is selling them and the percentage offered by the seller to the affiliate.

But what is actually involved in affiliate marketing? What do affiliates do on a daily basis? How do they earn money and how do they learn what to do?

1.   How Can I Get Started As An Affiliate?

Affiliate marketing is huge. There are thousands of people already making their main source of income from the internet. To get started as an affiliate you need to learn some basic strategies and build various methods of generating traffic from the internet to those offers. A lot of affiliates start with a simple blog.

2.   How Long Does It Take To Make A Living?

Some people go into affiliate marketing with the intention of creating a second income. Some people want to make big money. Depending on how much time you can dedicate to your affiliate business, and how dedicated you are to it, is a big factor in determining your results. Results vary from person to person. With a large advertising budget and the right business model, some affiliates have replaced their living in 6-12 months. For others it can take years before it replaces their existing income. Depending on your approach, advertising budget, and business model, it can take between 3 months and several years to build it to a point where it can replace an existing income.

3.   Can Anyone Do It?

One of the great things about affiliate marketing is that the technology is now available to allow anyone to build their own online business. As long as you are prepared to learn and implement that knowledge, anyone who can operate an email, can use online platforms and tools to build their own online business. The main thing you need is the desire to learn. Affiliate marketing isn't for everyone though. It does take a lot of hard work and it can take years before you are rewarded financially.

4.   What Are The Pitfalls Of An Affiliate Business?

You need to dedicate some time to your affiliate business for it to work for the long term. Some people go into affiliate marketing thinking it is some magic pill which will pay them instantly in cash. Much like a job you can't expect to get out more than you put in. Affiliate marketing is performance related. This means you don't get paid unless you can successfully sell products and services online. If you don't know what you are doing it can take years to do this. You can't be a dabbler and expect to earn the big money. The big earnings are created over years of hard work. Don't expect to achieve this with only a small amount of input.

5. What Are The Best Things About Affiliate Marketing?

Affiliate marketing offers an incredible amount of flexibility and freedom. You can work an affiliate business from anywhere in the world providing you have a laptop and an internet connection. You can choose your own hours and build it up around existing work. Many people come into affiliate marketing because it offers this kind of flexibility. They can choose their priorities in life: spend more time with family, choose your working hours, travel and work abroad. No more commuting to work or working long hours for a boss you don't like.

Affiliate marketing also offers incredible scalability. A business which is local is always limited to the people who can travel to that business. An online business can be global. Using digital products in conjunction with a global reach, you can scale using tools and software to reach thousands of people through digital technology. By using automation much of the work involved with an online business can be pre-built. By building automation into the business model, you can focus your activities on reaching a larger audience through content creation and paid advertising.

6. Why Am I Struggling With My Affiliate Business?

A lot of people struggle with their affiliate businesses. This can be for a number of reasons. Firstly building up an affiliate business takes time. You need to dedicate a lot of time to an affiliate business in the first place. Only when you reach a 'tipping point' do you really start to see your progress. Many affiliates simply don't realize how much work is involved. They underestimate how much time they need to dedicate to their online business to make it work.

Paid advertising can allow you to grow your affiliate business quickly. But it costs money and you need the right products too. You can't advertise small value items with paid advertising. You won't generate enough profit to cover your advertising costs. You need a range of products and an email list to advertise through.

Content marketing takes much longer to work, depending on your chosen area of business. If you find an untapped niche to market your blog in, you can make some fast progress. However, with a competitive niche you will struggle to get noticed above all the other content which you will have to compete with. There's several reasons why you might struggle. The main one is lack of knowledge. Get the right education first and your affiliate business will move much faster.

7. What's The Best Affiliate Model To Use?

There are many different affiliate models, all offering something different to suit the individual. Some affiliates target search traffic and aim to get their content found on Google. Some create their own products and sell them directly to customers. However, having a range of products which you can sell over and over to existing customers is a great model for long term success. Selling a single item online is limited. It means you can only make one commission from each sale. By choosing membership products to promote which also offer back end sales and a built in sales team, you can benefit from monthly commissions and up-sell commissions for the lifetime of any given customer. Selling membership products is definitely a game changer when it come to affiliate marketing because you make an income from each customer, rather than a single commission. But a good model to choose is one in which you have a passion for and can keep doing for the long term. Choosing products which you have no interest in is a short sighted plan. Think about what you would like to do online to generate an income. If you choose to go with your passion, your business will last much longer, and be more successful.

8. Can I Just Sell My Own Products?

Many affiliates create their own products to sell online. However, when you are starting out it is a good idea to learn the basics of marketing first. That way you can start earning more quickly from your affiliate business. I spent a long time creating my own products when I first discovered affiliate marketing. But I didn't sell anything because of a couple of reasons. Firstly I didn't research whether my products would have a big enough demand.

Secondly I didn't know how to market them. By joining a program which teaches you how to market products first, you can start making money more quickly. Don't waste time creating products if you don't know how to sell them. Marketing is a much more important skill for making money online. Once you know this skill, you can then apply it later when marketing your own products and services. Also your own products will be limited in range. By using an existing product range, you can benefit from products which are already selling. You can choose a program which offers high ticket commission, monthly memberships, back end sales and a built in sales team. Building your own products which offers all of these things not a possibility for most people when starting out.

The Difference between Affiliate Marketing and MLM Marketing

Affiliate Marketing is more like working as a sales representative. You have a position with a business and your job is to promote the product or service and close the sale. A good affiliate marketer is someone who likes to copy, paste, and post ads.

The MLM business model is much different. It takes real entrepreneurship to become successful. This is not a business model that one can copy, paste, and post and expect any kind of success. MLM or Relationship Marketing as it's commonly called these days takes a lot of work.

Listed below are a few of the requirements and skills needed to grow a successful MLM Business.

First you must be willing to be trained. Each MLM Company has its own policies and procedures manual and no two are exactly alike. So before even beginning your business read over these documents very carefully.

Second you want to learn as much about the product as possible. You do not want to make the mistake of not knowing the benefits of your products and how they can add value your prospective consumer.

Third you want to contact your up-line sponsor or if they aren't available or are new to the business, then find a team leader. You need someone with knowledge to guide and direct you. But more importantly you need to want to learn.

The criteria for any business regardless if that business operates totally as an off-line business, or an on-line business or as both, you want to know how to recruit people to grow a down-line team.

MLM business models thrive on growing a good solid down-line. And the down-line must be taught that unless the product sells, then there is no volume.

In most MLM business models, the down-line volume bonus is where the residual money is being made. So, product sales as well as recruiting new members are absolutely the fuels needed to drive the MLM business model engine.

I like to think of it this way, the sale of the product is the gasoline for the engine and the recruiting of members is the oil that lubricates the engine and keeps it running smooth. Take the time to study the difference between the two business models, before you take the leap of faith to join. It can mean the difference between success and failure.

How to Succeed on Social Media

One of your number one tools as an affiliate marketer is social media. This gives you a direct line of communication while at the same time letting you leverage the power of real world social networks. Compared with e-mail marketing, social media has the drawback of meaning you have to go through a third party - that being Facebook, Twitter or Google. But while this can be a problem, the positive side is that people can share your content with their friends and this gives it the potential to go viral. At the same time, social media is generally more multimedia and makes it easier for you to share different types of content. But unfortunately, 90% of businesses and marketers go about their social media marketing in entirely the wrong way. The problem here is that they will spend their time posting to social media but all they'll post about is how good their business is and it will sound very much like 'corporate speak'. If this is the type of status you are publishing to your Twitter or Facebook account, then unfortunately you are entirely missing the fundamental objective of social media marketing. This type of content would be fine of course, if you already had an audience and your objective was simply to market to them. What's actually happening here though, is that you're posting content to nobody and you're not giving anyone who might stumble upon it any reason that they should consider signing up. The question to always ask yourself when creating content for the web is: would you follow it? If you saw a social media account like this, then would you subscribe? If the answer is no, then you really need to reconsider how you might be providing your value.

How to Do Social Media Right

The key is all in the way that you look at your social media and the way you consider it within the broader context of your marketing. Specifically, it's important that you start to think of your social media profiles not only as an opportunity to promote yourself but actually as a product in its own right. What does that mean? It means that the social media accounts should provide value to the point where people want to sign up to them and would be disappointed if they were gone. Of course you need to do this while also remaining on-point with your marketing and that means you need to focus on whatever niche or industry you've chosen. If that's fitness, then it's no good for your Facebook account to be all about business. But it's also no good for your account to be all about how good the product you're selling is. Instead, you should aim to fill it with inspiring images of people working out and getting into great shape, with interesting industry news about genuinely fascinating new products and with helpful tips and advice. If you're selling life insurance, then you may find that it's a little harder to see how you can maintain an interesting and entertaining social media account. In that case though, you simply need to think a little more out of the box. In particular, this could mean that you share pictures of families enjoying life together, or tips for family activities. Maybe you could run a social media account about 'tips for the modern parent', or maybe you could give it a humorous angle 'dispatches from the frontline of parenthood'. Either way, you've now created almost a new brand, a new mission statement and a new form of value for that social media account itself and you've given people good reason to follow you.

This is how you then build your following and you would find that if you consistently put out good quality in this vein, it would eventually give you a huge audience to market to.

Affiliate Marketing Traffic Generation Strategies

Most of the times, Internet marketing beginners underestimate the real importance of sending direct and targeted site traffic to their merchant sites. This occurs because all the excitement of beginning a new affiliates marketing business.

Generating targeted traffic is the main job as an affiliate marketer, thus the only way of generating money by that scheme is by doing it on a consistent basis. If you analyze it, the merchant already did what is known as "heavy lifting": create the products, provide marketing support tools and offer attractive commissions. Everything is ready for you, so you're the main start of the movie now, you need to find the audience and convert them into customers.

So, now you are thinking about the steps are for getting that people, necessary to click your own affiliate links. Moreover, you don't know if you're capable of doing it. The good news is that, regardless of the background you have, I'll provide you the successful formula for traffic generation. Here are the steps you need to take:

1.   Defining and Researching Your Audience.

Identifying your target audience is crucial, if you don't do this at the beginning, you'll lose time and energy driving the wrong people to the wrong products, thus your affiliate sales numbers will suffer the same way. All you need to do is figure out what kind of products will give your audience the best value. This can be achieved by asking yourself the following questions:

a.   Who are the best clients?

b.   What are their emotional and physical details?

c.   What is the "language" they use? Intellectual or casual?

d.   What's the topic they enjoy talking about?

e.   Who do they admire?

f.   Have the brands and personalities a relationship?

By having the best answers of these questions and also knowing who you market is and what they want, you'll have a better chance of matching these people to the products and services you are selling. Most likely, they'll be interested in purchasing them.

1.   Giving a main reason to people to visit your sites and pay attention to you.

All niches, even the small ones have competition, thus you

need to offer people good reasons to devote some time to what you're offering. Notice that it has to be something that differentiate you from other thousand of affiliates selling the same product. Maybe the style you use may appeal to others. There are affiliates, for example, that build a strong reputation by being empathetic and/or conversational to their audience, in a way it generates trust.

There are other, for example, that show deep knowledge of the niche they are promoting. One excellent way to work this way is by start a blog and provide valuable free content to your listeners.

Another very good strategy is by building your email list. This allows you to follow up with the people who visit your site. You establish a relationship with them. They will know, like, and trust you. Once you have a very good mailing list of interested subscribers, you can promote multiple relevant products, thus increasing your profits per visitor.

2. Delivering excellent content that generates results for your Audience.

It's known that very good content is the foundation of a very successful affiliate marketing businesses; the reason of this is that it really highlights your very own personality and also knowledge of a niche. Anyway, in order to have it working, avoid repeating the same things other internet marketers do. The Internet is flooded with this information, thus it's worthless if you repeat it again. Here are some tips that will help you:

a)   Be Always honest: having a good reputation is definitely crucial, so that have long termed affiliate success. Make sure you avoid exaggeration. Promote the products that will really help your target audience.

b)   Your content needs to add value to your audience, so don't waste their time.

c)   Good copy writing is very important, so don't hesitate to explain in detail the features of the products you are promoting.

Affiliate marketing is for sure an excellent way to make money online, but it's not the only way, make sure to research all the range of possibilities, in order to increase your income as a marketer.

Myth of affiliate marketing

1.   Anyone can sign up for affiliate programs without a plan of action, and start making a ton of money!

Sorry! Nope, it does not work like that at all. The fact is that being an affiliate requires a deep level of dedication and time management among other skills.

2.   Affiliates can be successful without having a website for product information and related content.

This is another nugatory. Affiliates need a website or blog in order to offer regular content and or information relating to your affiliate products. A website brands YOU! Your traffic will begin with those that read and trust your opinions and recommendations.

3.   Simply placing buttons, banners, and ads on a webpage will drive your profits.

This myth is not true either! Scattered ads across websites, unless done properly displays clutter, not to mention that it does not show authority and knowledge by the affiliate unless you are both discussing and displaying related content as well as knowledge of the product.

4.   It is acceptable that affiliates can have any kind of influence or gain rapport with their audience without creating lists.

That is the wrong mind set there again. It's easy to clutter a website with potential money making links, but the difficult part is establishing trust and rapport with your target groups. As affiliates, we too are competing for customers. Rapport must be grown with clientele.

5.   If the product is great, the affiliate can sell it without much effort in content, strategy, or a good marketing plan.

Good content, trust, and building rapport. It's important to follow strategies that are proven to work for super affiliates. Isn't that the goal?

6.   Promoting products that have nothing to do with the content and categories of your website will yield substantial commissions.

Quite the opposite. Posting irrelevant products compared to our content or niche looks hungry and misinformed. It does not make you look professional or knowledgeable. Affiliates need to promote only what they know and only products related to what their website is supposed to be about. I am still cleaning some of these mistakes of my own up.

7.   Affiliates do not have to create a "brand" in order to thrive.

Although it is not always simple, heck, it's never simple to gain the trust as an expert in your niche; it is doable with some knowledge though. Build trust knowledge and rapport and you are branding!

8. An affiliate can earn good income with just a few websites without expanding and growth.

Super affiliates distinguish from the rest because they update, rebuild and reinvent their strategies continuously to the growing needs of the market.

These myths are simply not true. If you believe any one of these mythical ideas does not apply to you, you will be merely setting yourself up for disappointment. The fact is, if you build it, they will not come, until of course they trust you and your word about products you promote or recommend. Remember that that requires building rapport, and knowing your products.

Once you as an affiliate get these mythical ideas out of your thinking process, and have a good, detailed plan of action established, you will be on your way toward success as an affiliate.

Reasons people fail in affiliate marketing

So why do many people still fail in affiliate marketing?

The most critical aspect in the affiliate program is advertising. It is the most important thing all other kinds of business as well; many affiliate marketers fail in th s aspect because they lack hard work. Although it pays to be lucky, you cannot merely rely on it. Affiliate marketing isn't as simple as directing customers to the business site.

You must invest in yourself

If you want to earn big, of course, you have to invest time and great amount of hard work in promoting the products. The competition is very high and customers nowadays are very wise, too, as earlier mentioned. After all, who doesn't want to get the best purchase? That is, to pay less and get more in terms of quality and quantity.

Being prepared is critical in affiliate marketing

Lack of preparation is also a reason why one fails in affiliate marketing, whether he is a merchandiser or an affiliate. Part of the preparation is researching. On the part of the merchant, he has to be highly selective in choosing the right affiliate websites for his affiliate program.

In order to be sure he has the best choices, he must have exhausted his means in looking for highly interested affiliates whose sites are sure fit to his products and services.

The affiliate site's visitors must match his targeted customers. On the other hand, the affiliate marketer must likewise research on the good-paying merchandisers before he signs up for an affiliate program.

He must ensure that the merchant's products and services match his interests so he can give his full dedication and attention to the program.

He can get valuable information by joining affiliate forums, comparing different affiliate programs and reading articles on affiliate marketing where he can get tips from experienced affiliate marketers on how to choose the best merchants and products with high conversion rate.

Your website is critical to the success of your affiliate business

The website is a very important tool in the whole affiliate program. You should plan how your site is going to be, from domain name to the design, the lay-out, the content, and ads, as a marketer.

Some users are particular about what they see at first glance and thus when they find your site ugly, they won't spend their time looking at your site. On the other hand, there are those who want information more than anything else. Marketers with "rich-content" web sites are usually the ones who prosper in this business because the content improves traffic to the site.

Websites with high quality contents and relevant keywords are the best optimized sites. Having the right information about the product and service and not just a bunch of empty hyped-up advertisements will allow you to earn big in affiliate marketing even when you're asleep.

If you're not able to sustain the interest of your site visitor, you won't be able to lead them to purchase. No click-through means no sale and thus, no income on your part.

Selecting a top level domain name is also crucial to the success of the affiliate program. Lots of affiliate sites don't appear in the search engine results because they are deemed by affiliate managers as personal sites.

Major search directories and engines would think of your site as a transient one and thus, they won't list it in the directory.

Know first what you are going to promote, before you decide on the domain name. Even if they feature the exact products the customer is looking for, the customer might think the site is not relevant and becomes weary of the site contents.

An educated affiliate is a successful affiliate

Above all, an affiliate marketer must be willing to learn more. Certainly, there are still a lot of things to learn so an affiliate marketer must continue to educate himself so he can improve his marketing strategies. Many fail because they don't grow in the business and they are merely concerned about earning big commissions quickly.

If you want long-term and highly satisfactory results, take time to learn the ins and outs of the business. Continue to improve your knowledge especially with the basics in marketing ranging from advertising to programming, web page development, and search engine optimization techniques.

Likewise, study the needs and wants of your site users and how different merchandisers compete with each other.

If your initial attempts are failures do not give up. Keep plugging away. Do not get disappointed. You see, thousands are attracted by the possibility of generating skyrocketing incomes through affiliate marketing and so they sign up in any affiliate program without carefully understanding every aspect of the business.

When they don't get instant results, they quit and sign up for another program and repeat the process of just copying links and referring them to others. When you sign up for an affiliate program, don't expect to get rich in an instant.

Work on your advertising strategies and be patient. Stay focused and become the best student you can be and you will not be one that crashes in affiliate marketing.

Know Your Target Market When going into Affiliate Marketing

A crucial element to having success online when working a business as an affiliate marketer is to know your Target Market. That is to say, you need to know who, what and where your customers are.

When you understand your Target Market before you get into the nuts and bolts of your business then you save yourself time and money. You will also learn how to run your business on cold hard facts rather than running it on guess work and luck which is what most people in Affiliate Marketing seem to do.

The 3 main elements to Target Marketing are as follows,

1) Who Are You Attracting. You need to identify specific persons within your chosen market so that you can tailor your business to them. For example, if your market is Golf then rather than trying to attract everyone interested in golf go a bit deeper and target "lady golfers in the UK" or "Junior golfers".

Focus on the right people, give them what they want and you will have much better results.

2) What Are Their Problems. Now you know who they are you need to now know what their problems are within your market. If you identify their problems you will then be able to offer them solutions such as your Authoritative Website content and of course your affiliate products.

Using the Golf example, if you discover lady golfers have trouble finding equipment for their size then you now know that affiliate products aimed at this problem will be perfect to promote.

3) Where Are They. OK you know who your Target Market is, you know what their problems are, you now need to know where they hang out. Where do they visit online and in the real world. What kind of websites do they read, what real world places do they visit.

Understanding this kind of information will help you when you come to placing your affiliate adverts and the products you are promoting.

If you do your Target Marketing correctly then you will know exactly who your customers are. You will know exactly what they want to buy and you will know exactly where to place your adverts.

The Future of Affiliate Marketing As a Career Choice

Almost every kind of business today has an online presence and there are mechanisms that allow for online money transfers. It has therefore become very easy to purchase inventory, pay workers and receive goods and services without moving from where you are seated. The internet has made it possible for anybody to setup an easy online home based business.

Stay at home parents, students and senior citizens who still have the strength to work but are locked out from formal employment by their age can still live productive lives. Online entrepreneurship not only provides a platform for offering services to people in different parts of the world but also provides a steady source of income.

There are as many forms of online entrepreneurial activities as there are products and services to be sold. One of the most popular and fastest rising is affiliate marketing. The core principle of affiliate marketing is that the more people you covert, the more you earn.

You can start a career path in affiliate marketing with absolutely nothing in your hands. This means that you do not have to have product neither do you need money. Armed with just a computer with access to the internet, your first step would be to identify companies who have products and services to sell for a fee. By directing people to these companies' website, every sale made out of your efforts earns you an income.

With the benefits that affiliate marketing brings to an organization's sales, this is not a marketing tool that is going away soon. Companies like conversions made from affiliate marketing because it means that potential customers are made of the existence every day. The power that affiliate marketing has of word of mouth advertising is simply phenomenal.

Without leaving the house, affiliate marketing has proven that people can still make a decent living out of selling products that belongs to other people. It however takes patience and resilience to live off of affiliate marketing and people who have been in this field for a long time are witness to this. The best time to start is while still in school or before you become desperate for a source of livelihood.

There are many resources available on the web on how to start a career online. Many success stories of people who started and are reaping the benefits are also available to offer encouragement and insight into the dos and don'ts that build a successful career.

Becoming an Expert Affiliate Marketer

Nobody becomes an expert affiliate marketer over night. It requires a lot of work. If you don't know the basics on how to become one, then you are likely to never accomplish this feat. Fortunately, I am willing to tell you how to do this. The following steps will help you say goodbye to beginner's world of affiliate marketing.

1.   You need to learn the market. Look at what is going on in the marketing world. Follow the ups and downs of recent times. You should be an expert on what's trending at the moment. This is invaluable information. If you can really get a grasp on this, then you will be so much better than the competition. So, memorize the markets. Know people and know what they like.

2.   This information can be tricky to find. The key to acquiring this information is through marketing research. You will need to study people. You might have to put them in rooms with a two-way mirror and really watch them. See how they act and what they do. Put products in front of them and have them describe it to you. Study which words they say. Figure out what types of people describe things the same. All of this will be information that will set you apart as an expert affiliate marketer.

3.   All of this information can be gathered in a simpler way. I would suggest doing the research the old fashioned way. You are more likely to gain real information because you are studying real people. Still, if it is just too much work for you, there is a way to cheat. You do this through electronically gathering the information. You can do this by setting up internet surveys. You can also track people on the internet. Study what sites people are coming from before they come to your page. This is all information that is very important, and a lot quicker to gather.

4.   Never underestimate what businesses might be willing to tell you. Try to schedule meetings with executives in as many businesses as you can. Get to know them, and then ask them what they know about marketing. They have probably done tests like these a thousand times. If you butter them up enough, they might be willing to let you in on what they know. Be sure to write down this information. Sometimes standing on the shoulders of giants is the tallest we can ever get.

5.   Don't be afraid to go with your gut. After studying the trends for long enough, your gut will probably be pretty calibrated to actual trends. Now you can guess. Now Feature Articles, you are a professional.

The first is to define it in basic terms, much as you would explain a general business concept. One person is the salesman (affiliate), who promotes, markets and sells another person's (seller's) products or services for a specified commission per sale. The second is a more in-depth and involved answer, where you define it as a full-scale business, which requires time, effort and knowledge to truly grasp in its entirety. Considering the big picture, affiliate marketing is all about how you manage to bring in customers to buy the products or services offered by someone else

Mostly, the merchant provides all the tools that you need to market their products and services. Really, your job is to arrange traffic to their website and you get a certain percentage of that sale once a customer clicks on your link and buys. If you are starting out online, you may want to start with affiliate marketing first as there is no major expenses or outlay.

You are not responsible for developing the product or dealing with the customer as the customer will be directed to another website where all the essential information will be presented. Some people say that you don't need to know much about the product you are promoting. I beg to differ, if you are trying to promote this, you should at least be able to provide helpful tips and advice on the affiliate product you are trying to promote.

When you apply in an affiliate program, you simply worry about having traffic to your website, and then having them to click on your affiliates' links. You will earn cash when a person purchase the product of the affiliate using the link you provided.

A good affiliate program will provide you the necessary

tools, marketing advice along with keywords to help increase traffic to their site. The goal of the merchant is to get more links and clicks to their website so it is in their best interests to help you as you are spending the time to push traffic to their site.

However on a negative note, you need to remember that you are not the only one promoting the product. There are thousands of other marketers out there considering to promote the same product like you are. So competition is an issue that you need to deal with. Try to find an affiliate program that has a good reputation as some may decide to keep sales that you help made i.e. they may not pay you. So try and do research first about the product and cross off and affiliate programs they have a bad reputation.

The 24/7 availability, user friendliness and its reputation has attracted millions of affiliates from global destinations to Clickbank. For sellers, Clickbank is a place to find over 100,000 eager affiliates to promote and sell what they offer. Affiliates are allowed to pick and choose whatever products or services they wish to offer through their own websites, whether relevant to their particular field or not. The downside to using clickbank is that most of the super affiliates having usually dominated the search engines with traffic and SEO techniques to get that top page ranking.

One of the most lucrative options is to look for private affiliate programs. One way to do this is to do your own research into hot niche markets and look for products that don't have any affiliate programs attached to them. A hot niche market is one that high number of searches (at least 80 searches per day), low competing pages (around 30,000 to 60,000) and has Google Adwords advertisers in the organic searches. The only word of advice I can give you is spend the time to learn about affiliate marketing strategies so that you can put yourself ahead of the game. Learn from others who have products up and have been doing well in affiliate marketing.

Have been there before.

Ways to Increase Your Affiliate Sales

1. Become an "expert" on the product

The most successful affiliate marketers are "experts" on the products they promote. To become an expert, it's highly recommended that you purchase the product yourself to gain first-hand experience using it. If you cannot purchase the product, you must thoroughly research it until you become familiar and knowledgeable enough to promote it.

2. Participate in chat rooms related to the product

You can start your own chat or join an existing one. Do not try to selling initially, but during your chat, mention the product you're promoting and describe its benefits. If there is interest in your product, you can then refer them to the product through your affiliate link. The same concept holds true for forums and discussion boards.

3. Write your own affiliate program ads

Most merchants will provide pre-written ads for their affiliates to use. If you write your own ad, or make significant changes to the one that's pre-written, your ad will stand out from the others. Done properly, this will give you a great advantage over those affiliates that are using the same ad as everyone else.

4. Create a free newsletter or ezine

Submit your newsletter to the ezine directories and promote it on your website. Keep in mind that most subscribers are interested in receiving "information" that can help them. If you use your mailing list solely for selling, you will never gain credibility and will end up with a high unsubscribe rate. After you've developed a relationship and the trust of your subscribers, you can then recommend the products you are promoting

5. Create a free ebook

As part of your ebook, include an advertisement and a link to your affiliate website. The ebook can be given away free or used as an incentive to sign up for your newsletter. Submit your ebook to the ebook directories and offer it to other webmasters for inclusion on their website. The more exposure your ebook receives, the more sales you can make.

Reasons Why Affiliate Marketing Is The Best Way To Break Into Internet Marketing

Affiliate Marketing is the fastest, easiest, and most effective way to break into the Internet Marketing field of business and I also believe it is one of the best Home Businesses you can start. Reasons are given below.

1.   You don't need your own product.

The beauty of Affiliate Marketing is that you don't need a product to sell. There are plenty of merchants out there with plenty of products and they would be glad to pay you a commission to sell their products for them. That's what Affiliate Marketing is all about. Selling other people's stuff online.

2.   You don't need a shopping cart on you website.

With Affiliate Marketing, you don't need to place a shopping cart on your website. And you don't need to provide any means of accepting credit cards or processing payments either. With Affiliate Marketing, you just endorse the product you are selling, and provide a link (your unique affiliate link, of course) to the merchant's site.

3.   You don't have to store or ship products.

One of the biggest things that drew me to Affiliate Marketing was the fact that I didn't have to store or ship products. When I send a visitor to my merchant's website and they place an order, the merchant ships the product. I just sit back and wait for the commission. That is a sweet deal.

4.   You don't have to deal with customer complaints

Another big plus of Affiliate Marketing is that if a customer is not satisfied with the product he or she purchased they will usually go straight to the merchant to complain or request a refund. In rare cases, they may come back to your website and contact you through your information there, but that is really unusual. If they do come back to you, help them all you can. If you can't help them directly you can be a liason between them and the merchant. That way you can show your customer that you do, indeed, care about his satisfaction.

5.   You can sell anything you want to.

With Affiliate Marketing, you can sell any product you want to sell. Of course, you will want to sell products that are related to the theme of your Website, but the point is this. No matter what you site is about, you can literally find hundreds of products and merchants that will fit. There is no shortage of things to sell on the Internet.

6. You make money while you're not even working.

The beauty of Affiliate Marketing is that once you have your site set up and tweaked you can easily put it on auto-pilot. Since your merchants are the ones who ship the product and handle customer inquiries, you can sit back and relax and still make money. Of course, you will want to keep an eye on your site to make sure things are running smoothly, and you will want to add fresh content from time to time to stay friendly to the search engines, but it's a real joy to wake up in the morning, check your stats, and find out that you made a couple of hundred dollars while you were getting your beauty sleep.

Secrets to becoming a millionaire in affiliate marketing

Obviously, running multiple streams of affiliate marketing income is totally a great idea to grow your affiliate commission and online business. With those multiple sources of affiliate marketing income, you are running multiple affiliate marketing strategies at the same time. Also, you will maximize your profits online with those many affiliate marketing strategies. In this book, you will discover and learn basic steps to run multiple streams of affiliate marketing income.

With those steps, it is easier for you to run your own affiliate marketing business and build your own multiple streams of affiliate marketing income. You will leverage those simple steps and learn how to maximize your affiliate commission below.

Discover High Performance Keywords.

The first step is to discover high performance keywords for your affiliate marketing business online. With those high performance keywords, you will ensure that you can maximize your profits online and earn huge of affiliate commission. To discover the high performance keywords, you can use pay per click (PPC) search engine to test and find out which keywords are super-profitable and high performance for your business. Without testing systematically, it is difficult to identify which keywords are super-profitable and valuable for your home based affiliate marketing business.

Write Quality Relevancy Content with High Performance Keywords.

The next step for running success multiple streams of affiliate marketing income is to write quality relevancy content with those high performance keywords. You have to build your own original related to your market based on those high performance keywords. The highest recommendation is to focus on your reader's mind and the proper of writing.

Build Your Website Ranking Based on Your Content.

The next step is to upload your content given from previous step on your website. You have to optimize your web page with those high performance keywords as well. It means you must include those high performance keywords into your web page and content for your affiliate website. Also, there are many search engine optimization techniques on the internet to help you to build your website ranking in search engines.

Consolidate Your Content into Your Own Article.

The article marketing is one of the most effective affiliate marketing strategies to drive quality relevancy traffic to your affiliate website. All you have to do is to consolidate your content into the articles. You have to focus on writing, article layout, article structure and article formats. With those stuffs, it is easier for you to maximize the profits through your articles. Additionally, submitting your articles to other article directories is a good idea to build up your reputation and creditability. Also, it will help you drive more quality traffic to your affiliate website.

Post Your Articles into Your Blog.

To run the multiple streams of affiliate marketing income, bu lding your own blog with those same articles from previous step is a great idea. However, you have to customize those articles for your own blog. There is a different point between post messages in the blog and article. You have to put more your personality and be more personalized into your blog. For blogging online, you have to build up the relationship with your readers. That's why you have to be more personalized and socialized, rather than writing the articles.

Include Your Articles into Your Newsletter.

Providing newsletter strategies has proven that it is very powerful to drive more traffic to your affiliate website. Thus, to run multiple streams of affiliate marketing income, newsletter is one of the best strategies you should not forget. You can include your articles from the above step into your newsletter.

Participate in Forum through Your Articles.

Many studies reveal that participating in forums through your articles will help you boost skyrocket affiliate commission and grow your affiliate marketing business.

The highest recommendation is to use this strategy properly, rather than trying to sell your affiliate products in the community. You have to share and exchange the ideas and information related to your affiliate products among other people in the forums. That is the best way to maximize the power of forums and articles together!

Place Online Classified Ads.

The last step to run multiple streams of affiliate marketing income with multiple affiliate marketing strategies is to place online classified ads. With the content and high performance keywords from above steps, you can conduct your own online classified ads. The best approach to maximize profits from classified ads is to include properly your high performance keywords and benefits into your ads.

Final thoughts, it is important for affiliate marketing entrepreneurs to run multiple streams of affiliate marketing income. You have learnt how to combine several affiliate marketing strategies, like pay per click online advertising, search engine optimization, article marketing, blogging online marketing and email marketing, to run multiple streams of affiliate marketing income. The real key to your success for multiple streams of income is your creativity. You have to combine those affiliate marketing strategies together to maximize your profits.

Ways to Maximize Your Affiliate Marketing Program ROI

Affiliate marketing is not an easy task for the marketers to market the affiliate products successfully. But it's also not as difficult as most of the affiliate marketers typically earn well over six figures a month.The most important for every marketer is to build trust and relationship with the audience and consistently invest the time and effort.

While traffic sources are a significant factor in affiliate marketing success, the relevancy of the traffic is applied for all digital marketing and sales personnel. The key traffic sources can be SEO, social networks, blogging, email marketing, etc.

Digital products pay higher commissions than physical products as it requires least investment and effort to produce and distribute them. You can offer digital downloads to your readers like eBooks, audio/video files, software's, etc., without any additional overhead cost of production or distribution. You can also provide online, hosted and professional services for your local audiences.

What are the advantages of Affiliate Marketing?

Many online advertisers are looking for cost-effective ways to drive-in web traffic and secure their expenses. So,

Affiliate Marketing has several advantages like:

✓ Drives-in large volume of web traffic

✓ Helps you reach new customers

✓ Builds relationship with your audiences

✓ Gains a wider market place to sell products

✓ Can sell the products directly

✓ Track and monitor the customer behavior

✓ Easy to implement

✓ Low effort and low risk

✓ Doable by a single person

✓ Affiliate marketing campaign

In this era, affiliate marketing has expanded into a multi-billion dollar industry. Marketers around the world are using it as an effective marketing campaign. It's the right time to take action to grow your business and make money with affiliate marketing.

There are some important tips to make your marketing strategy more effective that would gain you more revenue with less investment.

Here are seven ways to maximize your perfect affiliate marketing program this year.

1. Identify your audience goals

The first step for every marketer is to know their audience's goals, interests, behaviors, etc. By understanding your audience's goals, you can find the products that will make them engaged or they want to achieve.

List your audiences emails and blog post comments

Send them emails and ask about their problems promptly

Look for solutions in public places like online forum sites to understand and assess the discussions on your topic.

2. Reach your audience goals

After identifying a desirable goal, you can gather some points to engage your readers and their needs for a specific product. It helps to coordinate your online marketing strategy.

Define your audience objectives

Select and find your target audience

Choose the right kind of platform that appeals to different audiences

3. Determine the tools and resources

There are several tools and resources that you can use to set up affiliate program partners and collect commissions. Some of the blogging and affiliate marketing tools can be used to sell your work and grow large audiences.

Collect emails to connect with your audience

Introduce your product or services

Find specific groups and list all the products that would help your audiences.?

4. Select a product to promote

Research for the best products that have affiliate programs and also meet your audience requirements. It's easy to promote those products that you know so that you can evaluate various issues from the user's point of view.

Promote a well-reviewed product.

Connect with the influencers to sell their products.

5. Setup and manage your affiliate program

Affiliate programs are an opportunity for you to get hundreds, even thousands of web sites all driving traffic to your site and making sales for you. It is based on your overall marketing strategy where you can setup affiliate program, manage and track the sales performance and more.

Analyze your competitors

Have a product that delivers promises

Provide affiliates with text links, banners, emails, articles, etc.

Track the sales

6. Promote your product

The fastest way to get quick results is to start promoting other people's products in return for a commission. There are several affiliate marketing promotional methods like PPC, SEO, coupon, Content, Social media, etc., that can be used for promoting your product.

Add affiliate links to blogs, eBooks, etc.

Create and promote custom content (write reviews, guest posts, etc.)

Craft promotional emails for other users?

7. Create an affiliate disclaimer page

Creating an affiliate disclaimer page on your website allows you to handle the commissions from products and services. So wherever you share an affiliate link, whether it's in web pages, blog posts or emails, let your readers know that you stand to earn a small commission.

The disclaimer must appear on any page

Must be mentioned that you receive compensation for any review or rating on your product

Disclaimer should be immediately evident to a typical visitor who views a review or rating on your site

Be Adequately Prepared For Affiliate Marketing

We all have to start at some point in time, and the majority of us starting off all chase that magic button that will turn your PC into an instant ATM. I know, I used to be a leading contender and grew quite fond of the idea having a few thousand dollar in the next few days. I live in South Africa and with the exchange rate we're talking a tiny fortune!

Terrible when that reality comes kicking you in the nuts and you realised you've been chasing that damn button for 18 months. Now what's "Instant" about that, nothing because you've been chasing so many promises instead of your dreams. Don't get confused between promises and dreams, it's the mother of all failures on the internet!

However, failure is also disguised as knowledge because you will learn to do something whatever you do online. And somewhere, someone is struggling with something you have already mastered. So, as an Affiliate Marketer the only way that you will stand out from an alarmingly large crowd and gain your audiences' trust, is to be able to engage any questions they may have about the product you are promoting.

This is why most marketers dread the idea of hosting and the research that comes with that!

Which is why your Blog is so important, because that is how you build a "Responsive Email List" with subscribers interested in your content. Your Blog becomes like a Social Signature where you share your knowledge and inspire your audience with useful content and tools. It's not always about the money, which will come when your content qualifies. Simple as that.

Where To Start

This question run through many beginners mind. Yoh have your response below

But Where Do You Start?

Glad you asked, and as you well know I love speaking WordPress with a little Google. Because that's the right place to start once you have built your product knowledge. Effectively you start by discovering your profitable niche, so you can target the keywords you wish to target in your domain name and site title. This is very important, so hold the horses on the domain and hosting if you have not done proper research. You may very well, quite sadly be wasting money.

I know I did and as a computer and device dinosaur (Back Then), it seemed even more so. It really is all about patience and research.

Take a moment and think about the things you love doing most and make a list because that's how you empower yourself to create unique content (No Where Else Available on the Internet). That's what Unique Content means, and without that you will reach snail speed at best. And that will be your "Profitable Niche", but why?

Because if you absolutely love what you do it will be impossible to give up, when you're truly fascinated by something you'll be unstoppable! Remember that super successful people are just dreamers who refused to give up, and nothing could make them stop. You know the saying "Quitters never win, and winners never quit", it really is how this works.

Once you have your niche, you must find the appropriate product to promote to an interested audience. Yes, this means you will actually have to purchase what you're about to present to your audience and personally test it.

Surprised? You shouldn't be because if you're seriously think you will become a dot com millionaire by not spending a single dime, then you are sadly mistaken. Not only must you be prepared to pay for training, you will also pay for hosting and that's a fact that must not be dismissed.

If an interested buyer asks you a run-down of what they're looking at purchasing, you must be able to respond confidently. People are tired of desperate sales pitches with hardly any info apart from promotional material provided to thousands of affiliates. Duplicate or "Scroll Over" content as I sometimes call it. Duplicated so many times there's not much uniqueness anymore.

Test the product to the extent that you can guide your interested audience even before they purchase. People like to know what they're paying for.

This all comes down to direction and focus, without which you may take a considerably long time to achieve your goals. It's all about tiny objective steps in the right direction, there's no such thing as a giant leap.

Some thoughts on making money in a few hours?

Now that's not even logical, seriously? If it was so easy to make millions online then economies would collapse... just let that sink in for a while. You must be prepared to face failure more times than you may later recall, and your level of achievement depends on YOU. What you put in, is what you get out.

Making money online as an affiliate marketer start with direction and there is no final destination, where little to no effort will bear the equivalent in fruit.

Yes, you may have seen some marketers sharing fancy screenshots but people are growing weary of these, and with good reason. Unfortunately this marketing tactic had become a little over exposed and borders BS by now, right?

Well yes and no. Because not all of these are bogus, but rather quite sadly misunderstood. The most important to watch out for is a full money back guarantee. In my opinion, someone not willing to offer you your money back may not quite have that kind of confidence in their product and neither should you. But that's just my opinion, don't want to trample any toes here... just a thought.

Now this coin has a flipside because the products you decide to promote should carry the same surety. Professional marketers call this the "Back Door" and it offers security and peace of mind. You will then have to wait the money back guarantee out before your commissions will be released to you. And there goes the idea of making money the next day, even if by some miracle you succeed in generating sales the first week.

The fancy screenshots from the guy willing to offer you your money back is an indication of what is possible with the system or product, not necessarily what is imminent. You may end up doing even better and it's all about focus, paying proper attention without rushing in an attempt to make money faster.

Conclusion

For individuals who are thinking twice about setting up an internet-based small business, think no more. The internet is that one place where you can make your business as competitive as the rest without investing so much. You only have to create a good website of your own and convert it into a more profitable one.

Before you can sign up for an affiliate internet program, you should already have an existing website which invites a steady flow of web traffic. This makes you attractive as a possible partner for an affiliate program, because you already have an audience on the internet.

To further strengthen your position and increase your bargaining power as a prospective partner, you should apply the most effective internet marketing techniques such as search engine optimization, brand marketing, and social media marketing which reach far and wide.

If you are a purely service website and you have no products of your own, that in itself is not a hindrance for you to enter into affiliate marketing. You don't have to create and feature your own product, because you have the alternative to select some of the best products which you particularly like to include in your website.

You can feature these products as a form of display

advertising which comes for free and with no obligations attached. Should there be any additional cost, it would be on the part of your partner. Your partner would be responsible for managing and maintaining his own website while you direct and send as many viewers and visitors to his site. It is up to your partner to translate these views and visits into actual sales through his own efforts at brand marketing.

You earn money from an affiliate internet program when you get paid a regular commission for all the business which you refer back to their site. For instance, for every new member you refer to your partner's site through article links and email marketing, you may get as much as a 30% cut in gross sales they make with this client. Your affiliate ID registers on your partner's database every time you refer customers through links and clicks on your website. These referrals can be tracked and analyzed to see how many visits and possible sales you are bringing into your partner's website.

If you are leaning towards the possibility of joining an affiliate internet program where you can participate in some forms of online marketing, then you are going in the right direction. Just learn as much as you can about affiliate marketing before you venture any further.

You need to discover your profitable niche, target your keywords and find the relevant products to satisfy an identified common need within your niche. You will spend money online, and may even end up losing some money if you want to make serious money in return. You will most definitely not become a dot com millionaire without spending a dime.

Accept that and prepare to learn instead of earn because a willingness to learn is the best mind-set to get you started, and ensure your success.

Secrets to Affiliate Marketing Residual Income

Let us first familiarize ourselves with the concepts of and residual income. What is a residual income? A residual income is a continuous income paid to you by a client. It has been said that it is the best source of income because it is a recurring income you receive long after your sale has been made. It usually comes in a specific amount at a specific interval, usually a month. Putting it together Now that we know what affiliate marketing and residual income are, let us put them together to create a single concept. The right affiliate marketing program will provide you with residual income for the duration of your customer's commitment. If you can make your program work into earning a huge residual income, you have developed one of the best ways of earning money without even having to work. The secrets in using affiliate marketing to generate residual income create a good marketing campaign. As any marketing strategy you use, creating a good campaign is a must. It is the key to every marketer 's success. A good marketing campaign is informative, as well as entertaining. This will keep your clients keep coming back for more. Set up a lead capture page. Many companies employing affiliate marketing offer income from referrals and of course, give commissions for every sale the affiliate company makes. That is why you need to create a lead capture page to build a quality prospect list for referrals. You can do this through employing an autoresponder. By using this, visitors can put in their names and email addresses to receive information from you. You can also create squeeze pages that give away free information or newsletters so that they will opt-in to sign up to your mailing list. When you have your list, you can send your subscribers ads to generate more sales and/or get commissions for referrals. Promote affiliate products or services that have recurring monthly payments. Another way to generate residual income from affiliate marketing is to get products or services that require continuous monthly charges. This is really residual income at its finest. Through this, you can earn money from a one time sale. You exert effort once and you will get paid over and over and over. Some of these products or services include membership sites and web hosting services. Build good customer relationships. You should always aim to build good customer relationships to get their loyalty. You can do this by making your approach personal and by tending to their needs. Always try to answer all your customers inquiries as to convince them to buy your products or avail of your services. Remember, loyal customers make big sales. There are other secrets to generate affiliate marketing residual income. But in the end, it all comes down to commitment of time, effort and hard work. You must understand that success in affiliate marketing and earning residual income does not come overnight. You will have to spend time, effort and a lot of hard work to create value for your business venture.

Summary

What is an affiliate program? Everyone who surfs the web has come across affiliate programs. You may have seen a banner on a website that says, "click here", and once you do, you get access to whatever's being promoted. Or you could click on a link in an email you've received. You're using someone's affiliate program.

Basically, the company that sells the product sets up an automated way for people to be paid a set amount to help them promote their products or services. The links send you to the company's website where you can buy the product. The owner of the originating website or email gets a fee for taking you there.

The bookstore Amazon was the first company to heavily promote affiliate marketing on the internet. Although this type of marketing is ideal for businesses that only operate online, it's also become popular with businesses that have both an online and bricks and mortar presence.

Affiliate programs are an ideal way to make your web site profitable. With the huge range of affiliate programs now available, there's almost bound to be something to suit you and your website.

The advantages for you

There's no need for you to develop the products – it's already been done. All you need to do is to pick the best out of those available. You don't need to spend money on making or storing the product. Sending people to your affiliate merchants means you don't need to take or process a single order, or worry about processing payments. You don't have to handle or mail the product - your merchants do that. You don't have to offer customer support. Affiliate programs are usually free to join. You can run your affiliate business part time for a little extra cash while making minimal effort.

Choosing your affiliates

It's worth spending some time making sure that you choose the right companies to affiliate with. Different companies have different requirements. Some require you to have a minimum number of visitors to your website, while others require you to have your own domain name.

The best way to choose an affiliate program that will suit you is according to the type of people who visit your website. If your website is about guitars, you're unlikely to have much success with affiliating with a company that sells gardening products. The first thing you need to do is know your target audience.

You also might consider whether you want to join every single affiliate program that comes your way. A lot of people find that they make the most money from using only a small number of programs. Also, concentrating your advertisements may allow you to be paid faster.

Sometimes, it can be hard to choose between two similar companies. What works well for someone else may not be the best choice for you. It's not just about how much money you can make – you'll want to feel confident in your recommendations.

You can maximize your income by thinking beyond the obvious. If your website is aimed at parents, obviously you might think of affiliating to a toy company. But what about books, clothes, videos, DVDs, child oriented software…

If you are thinking about affiliating with two similar websites, you might want to choose the one that easiest to use or offers the greater benefit to a visitor, even if it pays less in commissions. You'll do best with programs that represent a subject you're personally interested in. Your own interest in the subject will entice others.

To join an affiliate program, you simply go to the site and complete their online application form. Some programs approve you instantly, while others check out your application before it is approved. Once it's approved, you're given some HTML code that you can cut and paste onto your web page.

How do I make my money?

Before joining any program, you should probably be aware of the different payment programs available.

Pay Per Impression

Here you are paid according to the number of times the advertiser's banner is displayed on your site. The amount paid is usually small, but it is easy to earn as everytime a visitor loads the page, you earn. The more visitors your site attracts, the more you earn.

Pay Per Click

With this method you're only paid when visitors click the advertiser's banner on your site. It generally pays higher than the pay per impression program. You'll get better results if your banners are carefully selected to suit your target audience.

Pay Per Sale or Lead

You only earn if your visitors click through the banner and buy the product or service.

Often, to avoid wasting resources in issuing checks for very small amounts, advertisers will accrue the amount owed to you until it reaches a certain amount before they pay you.

How do they keep track of referrals?

Every affiliate banner or link that a visitor clicks on has some type of coding added to the URL - this differentiates it from other affiliates' links. The most common means of tracking affiliate links is by "cookies" Cookies are tiny files stored on your computer by a web browser when you click on an advertising link.

Cookies are generated to track visitors to websites. This is how they can "remember" what you bought when you visit there again. For an affiliate company, the cookie records information on which affiliate referred the visitor to the company, and when.

As some computer users block or delete cookies, there are other methods used to track referrals. For example, CGI-based scripts related to the individuals affiliate code attached to the URL links and database matching algorithms are used.

Second tier programs

A two tier program allows you as an affiliate to sign up other affiliates under you. You earn a smaller commission on the referrals or sales that arise from their advertising efforts as well as your own.

This costs you far less time and money for each sale if some of them aren't yours. In effect, you have your own sales force and pay a commission to your sub-affiliates. Except that the commission comes out of the affiliate company's profits rather than yours.

The affiliate company benefits by a possible exponential growth of its sales force for no more effort on its part - you're providing that. It's not hard to recruit people under you in two tier programs.

A second level can be a great advantage to you as an affiliate. Even if you only spread the word amongst friends and family, you never know when someone who signs up under you will really take off. They could earn you a lot by their own efforts in spreading the word about a program. You might not get rich, but you'll get some welcome extra income.Amulti tier affiliate program builds on the concept of a two-tier program.

Not only can you earn from sub-affiliates, but you can also earn from their sub-affiliates, and perhaps their sub-affiliates. With a two tier program, you have an incentive to sign up sub-affiliates. A multi-tier program gives you the incentive to help your sub affiliates sign up others.

Is it for me?

If you have a website then there is guaranteed to be an affiliate program to suit your needs and audience. For minimal effort you can make your website earn money, even while you're happily sleeping. Perhaps it won't make you a fortune overnight. And it's true that no-one hands you money for doing nothing. But with some careful thought and planning Business Management Articles, choosing an affiliate program that fits in with your website and sells products that you are confident in is a straightforward way of increasing your income. And it costs you nothing.

Get started with affiliate marketing today and start making money.

www.ingramcontent.com/pod-product-compliance
Lightning Source LLC
Chambersburg PA
CBHW071705210326
41597CB00017B/2337